WILLIAM SUTTON

Trading in
Currency options

NEW YORK INSTITUTE OF FINANCE

Library of Congress Cataloging-in-Publication Data
Sutton, W. H.
  Trading in Currency Options.

Including index.
1. Financial futures.
2. Foreign exchange.
3. Hedging (finance)
4. Option (contract)
I. Title.
II. Title: Currency Options.
HG6024.3.S87   1988   332.64′5   87–31236
ISBN 0–13–925983–X

© 1988 by NYIF Corp.
A Division of Simon & Schuster, Inc.
70 Pine Street, New York, NY 10270–0003

Printed in Great Britain

10 9 8 7 6 5 4 3 2 1

New York Institute of Finance
(NYIF Corp.)
70 Pine Street
New York, New York 10270–0003

Contents

Introduction

Currency options are one component of the fastest-growing sector in financial markets: derivative products. This generic term encompasses the organised exchanges where markets are made in financial futures and options, currency futures, and stock index futures and options. The term also embraces the whole gamut of financial by-products which institutions offer their customers; these range from interest rate and currency swaps to options on swaps and future rate agreements; also included are the range of tailor-made products, such as over-the-counter option markets in US Treasuries, 'Ginnie Mae's',[1] Eurobonds, and gilts, as well as interest rate 'caps' and 'floors'.

Partly because of their apparent complexity and partly because of the arcane and specialist language used by proponents, but also because of the volatile nature of the underlying markets on which these instruments are based, derivative products have received a bad press. For example, anyone who reads the financial newspapers has heard of how a succession of computer-triggered stop-loss selling orders on the stock index futures market in Chicago apparently sent the Dow Jones Industrial Average plunging 500 points on 'Black Monday', 19 October 1987. The Press reported how, in early 1986, some US Government securities traders lost several millions of dollars through 'hedging' their long Treasury positions in the futures market during a sharp bond market rally, and how, 12 months later, US investment banks reputedly lost close to one billion dollars trading derivative markets in mortgage-backed securities and over-the-counter bond options.

Other factors have contributed to the markets' poor image; the size of business in some derivative markets, particularly on the futures exchanges, dwarfs that of the underlying cash market on occasion; even the very manner of trading which has developed in open-outcry markets is in such contrast to some more traditional trading styles; consequently,

---

[1] Government National mortgage-backed pass-through certificates.

this has led to such markets being compared to giant casinos. The implication is that many derivative markets are independent creations somehow divorced from, or even a source of distortions in the underlying security; that higher volatility is a direct result of the existence of such products; that, in short, the 'tail wags the dog'.

There is no empirical evidence of this, however. In fact the opposite is more likely the case. Derivative products have been developed as an attempt by users of the market-place to hedge and control their risk. The rise in information technology and the growing sophistication and internationalism involved in trading financial instruments has increased the potential for volatility in the underlying markets. The enormous size of capital flows and the large imbalances in world trade between major trading blocs has meant, for example, that the traditional economic analysis of foreign exchange rates, or of government bond or stock market prices, has little relevance to the trading horizons of most international investors. As participants search for trading opportunities in global markets dominated by 'hot money' capital flows, so demand for hedging products to reduce the overall risk has prompted the development of new financial techniques around the world.

In reality, therefore, derivative product markets are the direct result of market volatility, not the cause of it. In the 1970s, for example, the inflationary hike caused by the dramatic rise in oil prices led to explosions in volume in the precious metals and 'soft' commodity markets. Today, with comparatively greater price stability worldwide, turnover in the commodities pits has declined considerably. In the period 1979–82, short-term interest rate volatility increased substantially, largely due to a change in monetary policy by the US Federal Reserve Board which itself was a reaction to this inflationary surge. As a consequence the Treasury bill futures contract in Chicago, and later the Eurodollar futures markets in both the IMM and in London (LIFFE) recorded very large volumes; a normal day on the IMM in those days saw the equivalent of $100 billion of three-month interest rate futures contracts change hands. Recently, with the greater stability of short-term interest rates and the corresponding rise in volatility in the world's equity markets, stock index futures have come to dominate turnover on the financial futures exchanges.

Similarly, in the foreign exchange markets, the unprecedented rise (1983–85) and subsequent fall (1985–87) in the US dollar caused major problems for corporate treasurers, international investors, and central banks alike. Windfall foreign exchange losses became enormous for the treasurer who failed to hedge, or who hedged too soon, or who borrowed money in the wrong currency; the investor in the Euro-currency markets quickly discovered that the risk of his bond position could appear insignificant relative to the movements which were occurring daily in his currency exposure. Currency options were a product of this enormous volatility and the demands from foreign exchange users for alternative hedging and risk management techniques.

Today on the main currency options exchanges in Philadelphia and Chicago some $2–$3 billion worth of business is transacted daily. Probably as much again changes hands on the inter-bank, or over-the-counter market, in the main centres of New York, London, Paris, Zurich, Geneva, Frankfurt, Singapore, Sydney and Tokyo. Although this figure is tiny compared to the vast scale of business in spot and forward foreign exchange (perhaps $150–$200 billion per day), the options market itself is only of recent creation, an infant still compared to the mature inter-bank market. Indeed, while commercial banks had been offering customised options to their corporate customers for several years the market proper, in terms of depth and liquidity, has been in existence only since about 1984. In reality, a genuinely efficient options market in terms of large size and competitive spreads did not develop until the second half of 1985. But given the understandable conservatism of many potential users, the apprehension shown by some central banks who have only very recently permitted some of these potential users access to the market, and the complexities of the tax and accounting issues in many financial centres, the growth of options trading in such a short space of time has been more than impressive.

The very word 'options' has unpleasant connotations for some would-be participants. The regulatory bodies in the United States, for example, took nearly fifty years to sanction the re-opening of commodity option trading following the scandals of the 1930s. Even today the word is redolent for some dangerous and highly questionable speculation. For such reasons the early marketing efforts of brokers, banks, and the exchanges encountered considerable scepticism and resistance from potential consumers of the product.

That the market has now gained general credibility, and that users of the market, who now number some of the largest corporations and investment managers, realise that options are, if anything, a conservative foreign exchange hedging tool and investment medium, is testimony in part to the efforts of these marketing teams. To a very large extent, however, acceptance has been forced on a market suffering from the effects of enormous volatility. The greater the risk, the greater has been the effort to manage the risk.

The purpose of this book is to explain some of the important concepts and illustrate some of the major hedging and trading uses of the currency options market. It is not a general introduction to the option market, however; several other publications have covered the many trading strategies available and the basic principles at far greater depth. Nor is this an academic treatise; although some discussion is included as to option pricing in general, my aim has been to write a primer for the market, a practical guide for potential users and not a mathematical textbook. Specifically, this is not a book about options, but about currency options. Obviously, some of the major techniques involved in the stock, bond, and foreign exchange options market will overlap; the essential product is not new, after all, and the building blocks of the market, call and put options, are the same whatever the underlying instrument. But perhaps because the market is relatively new there has been little analysis of the special problems and particular advantages of the currency options market. This is very much the emphasis of this book: to move behind the barrier of specialist language and technical terms which so often acts as an impediment to new business and to make the market more accessible to the potential user.

I would like to thank Steve Geovanis and Bob Sameth of Merrill Lynch for their many helpful comments (and constructive criticism). Also, thanks to Jeryl Hack, of Donaldson, Lufkin and Jenrette International, for making available charts on implied and historical volatility, and to John Padwater, of Northeastern University, for his assistance in writing the programs and producing the graphics for the section on Euro-currency money-market investments. Finally, and principally, I wish to thank my wife and children for running the house and home while I scribbled away for so many hours.

W. H. Sutton
February 1988

PART ONE

Inside currency options

'An option is an option is an option' – or so one would imagine. Yet terms that would seem to be in common use and well-understood for equity options, such as the definition of the very building blocks of the market, calls and puts, as well as the method of premium quotation, can be a constant source of confusion among potential users of the currency options market. Other difficulties abound; how much does the premium vary between American and European style options? Why in some cases are there large differences and in others none at all? Are the forward points included in the option premium? How much do changes in interest rate differentials effect the level of premium? How likely is early exercise of an American option? Why, for example, are deep in-the-money calls on Swiss francs very unlikely, but deep in-the-money calls on sterling very likely to be exercised early? Why are sterling puts usually more expensive than sterling calls, both struck at the spot? And why, in contrast, do Deutschmark call options usually trade at a higher premium than Deutschmark puts, again both struck at the spot?

The answers to these questions are not intuitively obvious and many new users of currency options blame any apparent discrepancies on anomalies in the market or to bullish or bearish sentiment affecting premiums. In either case the implication is that the market itself is inefficient or that in some way the odds are stacked against the user. Not surprisingly, a lack of understanding leads to a lack of confidence in the product. It is the purpose of this section to eliminate some of these misunderstandings.

As a preliminary to examining the 'nuts and bolts' of the currency options market, Part One also includes a survey of the markets themselves and a summary of some of the basic definitions.

CHAPTER 1

The market-place

For the origins of the modern market we have to look not to any of the major financial capitals but to the relatively obscure locations – in terms of the international foreign exchange market – of Vancouver, Philadelphia and Amsterdam. There, in late 1982, were established the first exchange traded markets in currency options. Today there are several major currency options exchanges around the world, although the level of turnover and liquidity varies from centre to centre.

The major currency options exchanges

The Philadelphia Stock Exchange

'Philly' currency options are the most widely traded and most active of the markets on physical (spot) currencies. Philadelphia is also the exchange most readily identified with the currency option product. 'American' style options are quoted on sterling, Deutschmarks, Swiss francs, Japanese yen, French francs, Canadian dollars, ECUs, and Australian dollars. In 1986 a total of just under eight million contracts were traded, with an average daily volume of nearly 40,000 contracts (equivalent to about $1 billion). Contracts are cleared by the Options Clearing Corporation (OCC), the largest clearing house in the United States.

The Chicago Mercantile Exchange

Options on currency futures are traded on the Index and Options Market (IOM), a division of the 'Merc'. Contracts are offered on all the major currencies with Deutschmarks being the most active – indeed the most active contract on any currency options exchange worldwide. (2.2 million contracts of Deutschmark futures options traded in 1986 at an average of 8,700 contracts per day (equivalent to nearly $500 million face value).) In total, the volume on the IOM closely matched that of Philadelphia in 1986 with 4.4 million contracts, but these were on average twice the Philadelphia contract size. The special feature of these options is not that they are 'American' style – that is, exercisable at any time – but that they are only exercisable into the underlying futures contract, not into the physical currency. Contracts are settled by the clearing house of the IMM.

Other centres

Philadelphia and the 'Merc' are the two major exchanges worldwide. There are other centres for currency option trading, however, but liquidity is lower and daily volumes are much smaller. A more comprehensive list of the exchanges and the more important contracts traded is given in Table 1.1.

Characteristic trading practices

The currency options exchange is a market-place where buyers and sellers of options meet to transact their business. Trading practices and conventions vary from market to market but all options exchanges share certain characteristics.

Table 1.1. Main exchanges and contracts: currency options.

Philadelphia Stock Exchange (PHLX)				
Underlying contracts	Contract size	Trading months	Settlement	Premium quote
Sterling	£12,500	Consecutive and quarterly[1]	Third Wednesday of month[2]	US $ per currency
Canadian $	$50,000 Canadian	,,	,,	,,
Dmarks	DM62,500	,,	,,	,,
S. francs	SF62,500	,,	,,	,,
F. francs	FF125,000	,,	,,	,,
Yen	Y 6.25 MM	,,	,,	,,
$ Australian	$A 50,000	,,	,,	,,

Notes:
1. Normally the first three delivery months are quoted consecutively and the following three months on a quarterly basis; e.g. in July, options are quoted for July, August, and September expires, and for December, March and June.
2. Options expire on the Saturday preceding the third Wednesday of the delivery month.

Table 1.1. continued.

Chicago Mercantile Exchange				
Underlying contracts[3]	Contract size	Trading months	Settlement	Premium quote
DM Futures	DM125,000	Consecutive and quarterly	Business day after expiry[4]	US $ per currency
SF futures	SF125,000	,,	,,	,,
B. Pound futures	£25,000	,,	,,	,,
Yen futures	Y 12.5 MM	,,	,,	,,
Canadian $ futures	CAN$ 100,000	,,	,,	,,

Notes:
3. Options are exerciseable into the underlying futures contract.
4. Futures options expire on the second Friday preceding the third Wednesday of the delivery month; the last trading day of the underlying futures contract is the Monday preceding the third Wednesday; the value day for physical delivery is the third Wednesday itself.

Chicago Board Options Exchange[5]				
Underlying contracts	Contract size	Trading months	Settlement[6]	Premium quote
Sterling	£25,000	Consecutive and quarterly	Third Wednesday of month	US $ per currency
Dmarks	DM125,000	,,	,,	,,
S. francs	SF125,000	,,	,,	,,
CAN $	$CAN100,000	,,	,,	,,

Note:
5. On 26 August 1987, all currency options contracts on the CBOE were transferred to Philadelphia; PHLX now offers, therefore, both American and European style currency options.
6. CBOE options are all 'European' style; that is, they cannot be exercised prior to the expiry date.

European Options Exchange, Amsterdam				
Underlying contracts	Contract size	Trading months	Settlement	Premium quote
Sterling	£5,000	March, June, September, December	First business day after expiry	US $ per pound
Dmarks	$10,000	,,	,,	DM per US $
Guilders	$10,000	,,	,,	NLG per US $

Table 1.1 continued.

The Montreal Exchange, Canada

Underlying contracts	Contract size	Trading months	Settlement	Premium quote
Sterling	£100,000	Consecutive and quarterly	4th business day after expiry	US $ per pound
Dmarks	$US 100,000	”	”	DM per US $
S. francs	$US 100,000	”	”	SF per US $
Yen	$US 100,000	”	”	Yen per US $
US $	$US 100,000	”	”	CAN$ per US $

London international financial futures exchange[6]

Underlying contracts	Contract size	Trading months	Settlement	Premium quote
Sterling	£25,000	March, June, September, December	3rd Wednesday of month	$ US per pound

Note:
6. The main distinguishing feature of LIFFE currency options is that both the long as well as the short option holder are margined.

The Stock Exchange, London[7]

Underlying contracts	Contract size	Trading months	Settlement	Premium quote
Sterling	£12,500	Consecutive and quarterly	3rd Wednesday of month	$ US per pound

Note:
7. The Stock Exchange currency options contracts are identical to those of Philadelphia; indeed, it is the intention of the London market to have fungible contracts with PHLX.

1. A public market

Traders meet together in a 'room', on a 'floor', or in a 'pit' to buy and sell options. The essence of the system is to encourage a market 'crowd' to develop which will foster healthy competition for business and hence encourage liquidity. By centralising trading in one area and making dealing visible, market practices which are either illegal or impediments to free competitive trading, such as price manipulation or 'rings', can be discouraged. The crowd is composed of members or members' representatives; some may be individual speculators who own seats and who trade options for personal profit; some, as on

LIFFE and Philadelphia, may be large commercial banks who perform the function of market-makers; and others may be brokers who only carry out customers' orders.

For similar reasons, the method of trading is public. On the futures markets (the IMM and LIFFE) the system is called 'open outcry' which is like a public auction process whereby all bids and offers must be audible to all traders in the pit and deals must be transacted on the market floor, not pre-arranged. On the securities markets (Philadelphia and the CBOE) the trading system is also one of open outcry with a specialist market-maker who guarantees to make a price with a specified spread and contract amount.

Furthermore, to emphasise the concept of an open market, all trading information and data is published and accessible to all. Financial newspapers print the previous day's market prices and trading volumes for the more active exchanges; news services such as Reuters and Telerate, give 'real time' data such as current bids and offers, times of the last trades and volumes.

Exchanges are owned by their members whose responsibility it is to ensure the proper functioning of the market. Some full-time, paid officials are employed by the exchange – in administration and marketing, for example – but the various exchange committees which are formed to run the markets are usually comprised of representatives of member firms. Their main responsibilities are the regulation and supervision of trading, the setting up of trading practices and standards, the establishment of contract terms and details, the collection of market date and settlement of trading disputes. The exchange is also responsible for providing machinery to settle trades and to guarantee performance of the contract.

But if exchanges organise themselves, they are, nevertheless, regulated formally, or otherwise by government bodies. A federal agency, the Securities and Exchange Commission (SEC) regulates Philadelphia and CBOE; another federal agency, the Commodities Futures Trading Commission (CTFC) regulates all futures markets in the United States and therefore has responsibility over currency futures options on the IMM. In the United Kingdom both The Stock Exchange and LIFFE were, until October 1985, self-regulatory bodies whose activities were closely supervised by the Bank of England. Today the two exchanges come under the supervision of the Securities and Investment Board (SIB).

2. Standardisation

On a busy day on the IMM some 200 to 300 traders will be crammed, sardine-fashion, into the currency option pits. For the open outcry system to work at all, it is essential for the majority in the pits to have the opportunity to trade the various options being quoted. Quite obviously, a multiplicity of strikes and maturities would at best diffuse liquidity and, at worse, cause chaos. In order to make such a trading system viable, all options exchanges have standardised and formalised the terms and conditions of the contracts traded.

For example, take the sterling contract in Philadelphia. All options are American style, there is only one unit of trading, the contract, which is £12,500. Premiums are quote in cents per £ with the minimum incremental move 0.05 cents. (Thus a premium might move from 1.25 cents to 1.30 cents but not to 1.27 cents.) Philadelphia normally trades six expiry months, the first three consecutive, the last three on the quarterly cycle (at the beginning of August, for example, options will be quoted for August, September and October and for December, March and June). A new series is added only when the old month expires. For each new series a minimum of five strikes are initially quoted, in 2.5 cent intervals around the spot. Thus with spot sterling at $1.50, strikes will be traded in the $1.45, $1.475, $1.50, $1.525 and $1.55 calls and puts. Only when the spot price moves through the highest or lowest strike will a new strike be added, in this case either the $1.425 or the $1.575 strike. Expiration dates and times never vary. Philadelphia currency options expire at 12 noon on the Saturday preceding the third Wednesday of the delivery month, although most brokers have a cut-off time on the Friday. Settlement procedures for exercise and assignment are also predetermined and established as part of the rules of the exchange.

Such contract terms may seem unnecessarily structured, yet every exchange options market is a compromise between liquidity and flexibility. Too many strikes or expiration dates and liquidity is diffused; too few and the rigidity of the market discourages new business. Any user of the exchange has to make the same compromise. For example, take the case of the treasurer of a small corporation who in early August, needs to buy $1.38 puts on £90,000 sterling expiring in six months. He can buy seven contracts, expiring in December or March, but not February; he can buy seven contracts (PDS 87,500) or eight contracts (PDS 100,000) but not 7.2 contracts (PDS 90,000); finally he has to choose between a $1.3750 and a $1.40 put. But in practice what he loses in flexibility, he gains in liquidity.

3. The clearing house

The credit risk on an options transaction is asymmetrical. A call option buyer pays premium to the option writer, giving the buyer the right to buy and the writer an obligation to sell a currency for the maturity period of the option. The credit risk from the point of view of the writer is nil once the premium has been received. The option buyer, however, is risking the ability of the writer to honour his commitment. On an options exchange, where liquidity depends on a large number of options contracts being bought and sold during a trading day, and where many of the members are private individuals, the idea of traders settling contracts between themselves would make the public auction system inoperable. Similarly, it would be an operational nightmare for traders who might buy and sell the same option ten times over and with ten different counterparties, but who finish the day's trading with a square book, to settle up individually at the close of business. Therefore, in order to facilitate the settlement of trades, all options exchanges have adopted a clearing house system.

The clearing house takes the opposite side of every transaction. It is the seller for every buyer, the buyer for every seller. As intra-day trading is always a zero-sum game (all profits and losses must balance), the clearing house settles all trades by debiting the accounts of the members who make losses and crediting the accounts of those who made profits. Overnight positions are handled differently; while option buyers pay the full premium to the clearing house in the normal way, option writers, for whom a credit risk exists from the point of view of the clearing house, cover this risk by paying margin.[1]

The margining system is the basis of the way the clearing house functions. Instead of receiving premium, the option writer will put up the premium plus extra funds to cover the risk of adverse overnight movement. This is known as initial margin and is akin to a performance bond in that the margin money is only temporarily put up with the clearing house. Once the position is closed out, possibly even the following day, all initial margin is returned to the option writer. But if the 'short' option position is run for a further day and if the market moves against the writer (the currency rallies, for example, when a call has been written), then further margin, known as maintenance or variation margin, is collected. By adjusting the margins daily according to the market levels (marking to the market), the clearing house is therefore able to protect itself against 'normal' market risk. When abnormal market moves occur and when, as happens very occasionally, the member is unable to meet his margin call and goes into default, the clearing house is able to guarantee the contract by virtue of the margin money it has collected from other members and from its own reserves, which are substantial. When necessary, it is empowered to

---

[1] The LIFFE exchange differs from all others in that it has a margin system for option buyers as well as writers.

call on other funds from its members to ensure performance of the contract.

In the United States, the clearing house of the IMM and the Options Clearing Corporation (OCC) – the body which clears all transactions on the securities options markets, on bonds and stocks as well as currency options on CBOE and Philadelphia – are both owned by their members. In London all options contracts on LIFFE and on The Stock Exchange are settled by the International Commodities Clearing House (ICCH) which is owned by the UK clearing banks, Standard Chartered Bank and the Royal Bank of Scotland. Thus the credit risk on the clearing house itself is the sum of its constituent parts, its owners or members. This is considerably less than the risk on any individual bank, however large its assets. The clearing house system, from an operational and credit point of view, is a corner-stone of market liquidity. While without it an exchange would be able to function, the volume of its business would be so restricted that activity in the pits would very quickly die away.

The exchange traded market: who uses it, and how to access it

The users of listed currency options can be classified into three groups:
1. Commercial and investment banks who use the exchanges partly for trading and arbitrage purposes but mainly to offset some of the risks in their over-the-counter books.
2. Corporate treasurers and portfolio managers who use the exchanges to hedge their currency exposure. Options are usually bought (writing is a comparative rarity) as an alternative to the spot or forward foreign exchange markets.
3. Individuals, both large and small who speculate on currency movements.

The percentage of business for each group is difficult to estimate. The average size trade on the exchanges is much smaller than on the OTC market, but this is more a question of trading practices in a pit versus the inter-bank market rather than a fair guide to the origin of the business. Many stock, commodity or currency brokers have access to the exchanges; also many commercial and investment banks handle regular business on the major markets, particularly Philadelphia and the IMM in the United States and LIFFE and The Stock Exchange in London. In order to trade some of the less active markets, Toronto, Vancouver or Amsterdam, for example, it is probably necessary to check around the market to see who trades what. Additionally, since commission rates are negotiable, it is important to find out the going rate and whether there is a discount for size or for spread trades etc. Documentation, usually in the form of a risk disclosure, statement and, where appropriate, a corporate authorisation to trade, is normally an obligation of most exchanges and should be completed before entering the first order.

The over-the-counter currency options market

Side by side with the exchanges, there has developed a highly liquid market in OTC currency options. Many commercial, investment and merchant banks make up the market which exists in all international financial centres, but especially in New York and London. Banks trade options with their customers but an active inter-bank market has also developed linked by several specialist currency options brokers. Volume in the OTC market, as in the spot or forward markets is difficult to estimate but guesses have put average turnover at anything from half to twice the business done in the exchanges which itself is about $3 billion a day. The over-the-counter market is, by definition, offering a tailor-made product to potential users; there is no standardisation of terms, either for expiration dates, strikes, exercise procedures or even for the method of quoting premium. The essence of the market is flexibility; banks will endeavour to make prices in any currency, any strike, any maturity. Some banks, such as some of the UK clearers, offer options in amounts in size smaller than the Philadelphia contract, in units of PDS 5,000, for example, to their smaller customers. But the normal market size is larger. In the inter-bank market the average size of trade is in about $5 to $10 million and deals in the region of $100 million and above are not uncommon. The OTC market is also able to deal in the odd-sized amount, not just round lots. This may be important for portfolio managers, for example, looking to hedge the principal and interest of a foreign bond investment.

Options have been traded with expirations of only a few hours, yet ten year maturities are not unknown. Liquidity is greatest in the one to twelve month area, however, and out further than five years, the market is more a matter of negotiation and matching up of counterparties rather than of liquid two-way prices. Some banks concentrate their resources on the major currencies, on the Deutschmark, Swiss franc, yen and sterling against the US dollar, which are also the most liquid spot markets. Others will endeavour to make prices in any currency. There is considerable business from time to time in ECUs, French francs, Dutch guilders and Canadian dollars. 'Exotic' currencies, such as Italian lira, and Australian and New Zealand dollars and some cross-rate options, particularly against sterling, have periods of great activity. Currency options business feeds on volatility, however, so in quiet periods options on the 'exotics' and on the crosses become less liquid. Banks hedge their option exposures in the forward foreign exchange market. Therefore, the only serious impediment to market-making is where there is no freely tradeable forward market in the relevant currency or where the spreads in the forwards are very wide (as in the long dates).

The OTC market differs from listed options in a similar manner to the way the spot foreign exchange market differs from currency futures. The differences are summarised in Table 1.2. The OTC market deals in customised options; the size, the expiration, the strike and the option type (American or European), are all negotiable. In the exchanges the terms are all standardised. The OTC market is a telephone market. There is no market 'crowd' (apart from other market-makers), deals are transacted between two parties, the bank and its customer, or between a bank and another bank. There is therefore no clearing house to stand between the two parties to the transaction, which means that the settlement procedures and the credit risk are matters to be settled by the parties concerned. In the terms of the exchanges, the OTC market is unregulated. However, all market-makers come under the supervision of the central bank as with all foreign exchange transactions. In London, for example, the Bank of England keeps a close eye on all activities of the market. Commissions on the listed market are negotiable; on the OTC market there are no commissions as such, the market-maker's spread giving him his 'turn'. Liquidity in both the exchanges and the OTC markets derives from banks and from corporates, but the listed market sees a much larger percentage of individual traders and private speculators. Finally, the over-the-counter market is a 24-hour affair. Unlike the exchanges, there are no opening or closing times, although liquidity obviously matches that of the spot market, so that trading activity during Far East hours, for example, can be very low, particularly as the options market itself is the least developed in the Far East. Some banks offer a

Table 1.2. Over-the-counter and listed options: summary of principal differences.

	OTC	Exchanges
Size	Negotiable	Standardised
Expiry	,,	,,
Strike	,,	,,
Option type (American or European)	,,	,,
Deal method	Telephone	Open outcry
Commissions	Net prices	Negotiable
Security	Case by case	Clearing house
Regulation	Self or central bank	Government agencies
Liquidity	Banks or corporations or portfolio managers	Same + individuals

24-hour service in options so that a deal done in London first thing in the morning can be closed out that evening in New York or early next morning in Singapore or in Tokyo.

In its earliest days, the over-the-counter market was thin and illiquid. Considerable arbitrage business was transacted between the OTC and the exchanges and the spreads (when banks made two-way prices at all) were wide. The lack of market liquidity and relative inexperience of some of the traders resulted in some spectacular losses for a few banks with the result that some reduced the size of their books and others withdrew from the market completely. One of the problems of the early market was that the majority of the customers were buyers of options. This created a large imbalance in most dealers' books at a time when the exchanges were too thin to support inter-bank sized transactions. Consequently market-makers were heavily exposed to erratic, unpredictable moves in the spot market such as were precipitated by the intervention of the central banks in the early weeks of 1985. However, the combination of the increase in the number of option writers, better liquidity on the exchanges and the commitment of a growing number of banks (in spite of large losses for some) to make prices, ensured the eventual success of the OTC market. To this list should be added the increasing sophistication of software packages designed to analyse option risk exposure.

The type of user most familiar with the OTC market is the corporate treasurer of both large and small companies, and the international portfolio manager. It is used by individual speculators and by financial institutions to take strategic or speculative positions in currencies. But its main purpose remains as a hedging medium. Access to the market, for the corporate treasurer or the large investor, is probably easiest through his commercial or investment banking connections, although several brokers offer a service on the over-the-counter market as well as on the currency options exchanges. Documentation is usually a simple for-mality. With customers buying options, the transaction is effectively riskless once the premium has been received (although there remains a risk of non-delivery on the exercise of the option). But with customers writing options, the risk is similar to that of an outright forward and is treated as such, banks normally allowing customers to deal up to their own delivery limits. Premium is usually paid spot value (two business days after the transaction) and margining of short options positions is unusual.

The exchanges versus the OTC market: the pros and cons

The main advantage of the listed market is the public auction system. The newcomer to the market can be sure that the premium he pays or receives, publicly negotiated and displayed on market screens and published the following day in the financial press, is 'fair'. Even without access to a market screen, he can trace his position by telephoning his broker and asking for the latest quote publicly displayed on Reuters, Telerate or whatever. His position remains confidential. When he liquidates, he buys or sells at the market price which again the public auction system ensures should be 'fair'.

By contrast, on the OTC market, where the contract is between the bank and its customer, the buyer or writer has no way of telling whether the premium quoted is fair or otherwise. And, as the bank knows his 'side', the suspicion will always remain that the premium the customer paid was too much, or on the writing side that the premium received was too little. Nor is there any method of monitoring the position because there is no public price display system on the OTC market.

There are some situations where the public auction system is at a disadvantage compared to the OTC market. For example, as liquidity is the greatest on the exchanges in the near-the-money strikes with medium maturities (two or three months), it may not be easy for a customer holding an option position which has moved deep in- or far out-of-the money to liquidate his position, particularly if the option has under a month to expire and the quantity is large. He will inevitably have to show his hand to the whole market and very likely find that the only trader willing to make a price is a bank or an exchange market-maker who will only take the other side of the trade if he can arbitrage the option with the forward market, or against futures. By contrast, the market-maker over-the-counter will usually make a competitive price for the whole amount, happy enough to close an outstanding position on his books on his side of the spread.

Another advantage of the exchange traded markets is the clearing house system. Primarily, there is the attraction of dealing with an organisation whose credit rating is above that of any 'AAA' bank. For banks and large institutions who trade currency options in 'size', the credit process in the inter-bank market can be a major inhibition to doing business. As previously mentioned, the credit risk on an option is asymmetrical; once the writer of an option receives the premium to all intents and purposes he has no further credit risk. The buyer, however, has a contingent claim on the writer for the duration of the option. Therefore most banks are relatively restricted on lines of credit with each other for option trading purposes. In addition, once those lines are 'full', not only is further option trading prohibited, but so may be more traditional foreign exchange business (loans, deposits, forwards) between the bank and its counterparty or customer. This creates two sorts of problems for the currency option trader. Firstly, not to use up his lines unnecessarily because it will restrict his own freedom of action and secondly, not to restrict other traders in the bank from carrying out their normal business. In the exchanges an option buyer is limited in the size of business he can undertake only by the nature of the amount of premium he can afford to pay (and by the liquidity of the market). But credit risk is not a serious issue.

At the other end of the spectrum, the traded options market presents the only opportunity to the small trader or the individual speculator to write options. For similar credit reasons, banks will rarely allow private individuals to write options to them unless they are covered by some form of collateral. The margin system on the exchanges allows individuals to write options in comparatively large sizes. The only restriction is that imposed by the clearing house member on his customer (which again is a credit decision).

The margin system can be two-edged, however; for option writers without the operational support to manage and supervise the system of daily margin payments or receipts, the administrative problems involved can be both expensive and time-consuming. The marked-to-the-market system ensures that losses are taken on a daily basis rather than on the expiration day of the option. However, the underlying asset against which the option may be written (a currency bond, for example), may not be valued on the same basis. This could result in problems in accounting as well as those in administration and in operations. Clearly, therefore, for larger customers with lines of credit from several banks, writing options over-the-counter, where no margins are requested and where premiums are paid away immediately, has significant advantages over the exchanges.

If the essence of the traded options market is simplicity (standardised strikes, maturities, amounts), this can also be a significant disadvantage for some market users. Corporate treasurer wishing to hedge a specific amount, strike or expiry date, or those needing flexibility to put together multiple option strategies, find problems in the rigidity of the exchange traded markets. The OTC market is liquid out to at least 12 months, and prices can be obtained in good size from 18 months to three years. Markets in even longer maturities can often be made, but the maximum maturity of exchange traded currency options is about nine months and liquidity is best in the shorter-dated options with near-the-money strikes. The exchanges only offer options on the major currencies against the dollar. The OTC market is the only source for 'exotics' or cross-rate options. Furthermore the very number of exchange traded currency option markets around the world causes problems for potential users. Principally this leads to a diffusion of liquidity (having two rival currency options exchanges in London and Chicago, for example, poses at the very least an administrative headache for the brokers), liquidity in Deutsch-mark options is probably best on the IMM, sterling options are best known in Philadelphia, CBOE options are European-style which may be an advantage, but so may the margining system on LIFFE. The London Stock Exchange has announced plans for its currency options contracts to be fungible with Philadelphia, however. This variety of choice creates as many problems for the trader as it solves. Different documentation may be required for each exchange according to the various regulatory authorities concerned. In OTC trading, because the market is relatively unregulated, and because a bank is often trading with an existing customer in foreign exchange or with an inter-bank counterparty, documentation requirements (certainly for customers buying options) are minimal. In any event, the major prerequisite of any market, liquidity, is not assisted by the large number of option exchanges. In addition the 24-hour nature of the over-the-counter market is a signifi-cant advantage over the restricted hours on the exchanges. A summary of the principal advantages and disadvantages of listed and OTC options are to be found in Table 1.3.

Table 1.3. Over-the-counter and listed options: advantages and disadvantages.

	Advantages	Disadvantages
Listed	Public display	Restricted number of currencies (no exotics or crosses)
	Confidentiality	No maturities above one year
	Clearing house (credit)	Too many exchanges
	Clearing house margins allowing individuals to write options	Margins cumbersome for some corporates or investment managers
		Restricted hours
		Documentation
OTC	Flexibility	Lack of confidentiality
	Ease of access	No price display
	No margins	Greater credit risk
	Easy documentation	
	Market hours	
	Longer maturities	
	Markets in most currencies	

Currency option basics

Call and put options

Any option market user is aware of the basic definitions of the product. A call option gives the owner the right to buy, and the writer the obligation to sell, a specific amount of the underlying security at a predetermined exercise price to a particular date. A put option gives the holder the right to sell, and the writer the obligation to buy, a specific amount of the underlying security at a predetermined exercise price to a particular date. With most securities this presents no problems. Thus the buyer of a call option on gold has the right to buy a certain amount of gold from the option writer; the writer of a call option on IBM has the obligation to deliver a specific amount of IBM shares to the option buyer. One potentially confusing factor with currency options, however, is that a foreign exchange transaction is an exchange of one country's currency for another; the buyer of a put on Swiss francs has the right to sell (deliver) a certain amount of Swiss francs and receive US dollars at the strike price (exchange rate). If exercise takes place the buyer will pay Swiss francs and receive US dollars; the writer of the option will receive Swiss francs and pay US dollars. This changes the definition somewhat.

Call option

The buyer of a currency call option has the right to buy (take delivery of) a predetermined amount of one currency in exchange for a predetermined amount of another currency at a predetermined date[1] and at a predetermined exchange rate.

The writer of a currency call option has the obligation to sell (deliver) a predetermined amount of one currency in exchange for a predetermined amount of another currency at a predetermined date and at a predetermined exchange rate.

[1] Strictly speaking, this applies to European style options which can only be exercised on the expiration date; American style options can be exercised at any time.

Put option[2]

The buyer of a currency put option has the right to sell (deliver) a predetermined amount of one currency in exchange for a predetermined amount of another currency at a predetermined date and at a predetermined exchange rate.

The writer of a currency put option has the obligation to buy (take delivery of) a predetermined amount of one currency in exchange for a predetermined amount of another currency at a predetermined date and at a predetermined exchange rate.

> Take, for example, a put option on Swiss francs against US dollars expiring 21 September 1988, for six million Swiss francs struck at a rate of Swiss francs 1.50 per US dollar.

> The buyer of the put option has the right to deliver six million Swiss francs and to receive four million US dollars; (SF 6,000,000 ÷ 1.50 = $4,000,000). The right expires on 21 September 1988.

> The writer of this put option, therefore, has the commitment to receive six million Swiss francs in exchange for $4 million. This commitment lapses after 21 September 1988.

The two examples given above are a source of potential confusion which again rarely applies in traditional stock or commodity option markets; this confusion is in the quotation method itself.

How currency options are quoted

> Example 1: Buy a 5 March Deutschmark call struck at DM 2.00 for 3.00%.
> Example 2: Buy a 5 March Deutschmark call struck at DM 2.00 for $0.0150.
> Example 3: Buy a 5 March Deutschmark call struck at $0.50 for $0.0150.
> Example 4: Buy a 5 March US dollar put struck at DM 2.00 for DM 0.0540.

The four examples given above all refer to the same option. Examples 1 and 2 would be likely to be quoted in the over-the-counter markets in London or New York; example 3 would be quoted by anyone using the exchange traded market; example 4 would be quoted by a Swiss or German bank in the over-the-counter market. There are two reasons for this apparent confusion:

1. As was mentioned previously, a foreign exchange transaction is an exchange of one country's money for another; the foreign exchange rate is one country's currency expressed in terms of another's. If the US dollar is rising against the Deutschmark, the Deutschmark is falling against the US dollar.

---

[2] The terms 'call' and 'put' option can be interchangeable in currency options; a call on the Japanese yen is, by definition, a put on another currency such as US dollars.

This begs one fundamental question; is a call option the right to buy US dollars or the right to buy Deutschmarks? The answer depends on the viewpoint of the user. In West Germany or Switzerland, where the base currency is Deutschmarks or Swiss francs and the foreign currency is US dollars, a call option means the right to buy the dollar against the base currency; a 'call' is the right to buy US dollars in this case. However, in virtually all the exchanges and in the over-the-counter markets in London, Paris, New York and Tokyo, the US dollar is the base currency and the convention is widely accepted that a currency option is on the foreign currency, the mark, the Swiss franc, the Japanese yen etc. This convention still applies when a currency is normally quoted in terms of dollars per currency (sterling, Australian dollars, New Zealand dollars, ECU etc.). This same convention has been adopted throughout this book. Thus a currency option, call or put, is on the currency itself, not the US dollar.

2. The second cause of confusion is in the quotation system adopted by different users of the currency option market. Given that the foreign exchange rate is an expression of one currency's money in the terms of another, the manner in which the rate, or in this case the premium, is expressed depends upon the convention of the user. For example, sterling is a currency which is universally expressed in terms of US dollars per pound ($1.60, $1.55 etc.); other major currencies however are normally quoted in what are known as 'European terms', as so much currency per US dollar (for example, DM 1.80, SF 1.55, yen 155). On the currency futures and options markets, however, all currencies are quoted in what are called 'American' or reciprocal terms, US dollars per currency.[3] Thus a $/DM rate of DM 2.00 (that is, two Deutschmarks per dollar) would be quoted $0.5 per Deutschmark on the futures and options exchanges. Similarly, a $/SF rate of SF 1.60 could also be expressed as $0.625 per Swiss franc.

Originally the 'American' style of quotation, US dollars per currency, was used extensively in the United States; now the 'European' convention is widely accepted for the majority of currencies although there are some, ECUs and Canadian Dollars for example, where quotes in either style are to be found.[4] Sterling, Australian and New Zealand dollars are

---

[3] Unfortunately this is another unavoidable source of confusion; 'American' or 'European' style refers to the way the foreign exchange rate is expressed – US dollars per currency or currency per US dollar – not to the type of exercise provision in the option itself. This is discussed in the next section.

[4] More commonly Canadian dollars are expressed as Canadian per US dollar, and ECUs as US dollars per ECU.

universally quoted 'American' style, US dollars per currency. The futures and options exchanges decided to retain the 'American' system of quotation throughout, however. The reason for this was two-fold; firstly, for commodity traders in the early days of the IMM, the 'European' method seemed illogical. This is because a trader who buys Deutschmarks at DM 1.90, for example, and later sells them at DM 1.95 is of course making a loss: e.g.

Buy DM 1,000,000 at DM 1.90 / pay $526,315 (DM 1 MM ÷ DM 1.90)
Sell DM 1,000,000 at DM 1.95 / receive $512,820 (DM 1 MM ÷ DM 1.95)
Net US dollar loss = $526,315 − $512,820 = $13,495

Foreign exchange traders have no problem adjusting to this convention, but commodity traders were unhappy with this quotation method. Consequently, they turned the quote on its head and developed, for them, a more logical system. According to the IMM style the trade would appear as follows:

Buy DM 1,000,000 at $0.5263 (1/1.90)
Sell DM 1,000,000 at $0.5128 (1/1.95)
Loss = ($0.5263 − $0.5128) × DM 1,000,000
= $0.00135 × DM 1,000,000 = $13,500

When rounded down to four decimal places the loss, $13,500, is the same as with the 'European' style of quotation. One alternative solution for the IMM would have been to have used the US dollar as the base unit; instead of 'buying' Deutschmarks at DM 1.90 the market could have adopted the convention of 'selling' US dollars at DM 1.90. The problem with this method is that the profit or loss would be in Deutschmarks rather than US dollars and when converted back into dollars would be inconsistent, for example:

1. Sell $1,000,000 at DM 1.90: buy $1,000,000 at DM 1.95: Deutschmark loss
    = (DM 1.90 − DM 1.95) × $1,000,000
    = DM 0.05 × $1,000,000
    = DM 50,000
    US dollar loss = DM 50,000 ÷ $/DM spot rate
    = DM 50,000 ÷ DM 1.95
    = $25,641.

But

2. Sell $1,000,000 at DM 2.90: buy $1,000,000 at DM 2.95: DM loss = DM 0.05 × $1,000,000 = DM 50,000: US dollar loss = DM 50,000 ÷ $/DM spot rate: = DM 50,000 ÷ DM 2.95: = $16,949.

The Deutschmark profit or loss is consistent (DM 50,000) but the US dollar equivalent varies according to the $/DM spot rate. It was vital for the exchanges to have a unified quotation system so that the 'tick value', the value of the minimal incremental move, was a constant figure in US dollar terms. Only in this way could systems allow for consistent initial and variation margin calls. On the IMM the minimum incremental move for Deutschmark futures and options contracts is $0.0001. With a contract size of Deutschmarks 125,000 this translates into the following US dollar values:

IMM futures and options tick value: DM 125,000 × $0.0001 = $12.50

This is also the contract size and tick value for the Deutschmark option contract on CBOE. On Philadelphia and on the London Stock Exchange the contract size is DM 62,500 and the minimum incremental move also $0.0001. There the tick value is:

DM 62,500 × $0.0001 = $6.25

Thus calculating premium amounts on the exchanges or over-the-counter is relatively straightforward using the reciprocal system. Returning to examples 2 and 3:

2.   Buy a March 5 Deutschmark call struck at DM 2.00 for $0.0150
3.   Buy a March 5 Deutschmark call struck at $0.50 for $0.0150

Example 2 would be used in the OTC market where European style quotes predominate (DM 2.00 per US dollar); example 3 would be used on the exchanges where the strike would also be expressed in reciprocal form ($0.50 per DM). Assuming that the underlying amount in both cases was DM 1,000,000 the premium cost in both examples would be the same:

DM 1,000,000 × $0.0150 = $15,000

Were example 3 to have been executed on the IMM or CBOE the transaction could be written as follows:

Buy 8 contracts (8 × DM 125,000 = DM 1,000,000) DM calls struck at $0.50 for $0.0150.

On the telephone, with the trader talking to his broker, the order would be expressed:

'Buy 8 IMM (or CBOE) March fifty calls for 150 points'.

The premium is calculated as follows:

Either a) DM 1,000,000 × $0.0150 = $15,000
or, more commonly, b) 8 × $12.50 (tick value) × 150 (number of points) = $15,000

On Philadelphia or on the London Stock Exchange the contract size is half that of the IMM or CBOE. Therefore the same transaction would involve buying 16 contracts (DM 1,000,000 ÷ DM 62,500 = 16). The method of calculating the premium would be the same, however:

16 × $6.25 (tick value) × 150 = $15,000

In example 1 the premium amount is also the same but the premium is expressed as a percentage of the strike:

1. Buy a March 5 Deutschmark call struck at DM 2.00 for 3 per cent.

Percentage of the strike means 'percentage of the US dollar amount through the strike'. The simplest method of calculating the premium is to convert the underlying amount into US dollars and then multiply by the percentage amount:

DM 1,000,000 ÷ DM 2.00 (strike) = $500,000 × 3% = $15,000

Remember that on exercise of the option the amount of currency to be paid or received depends only on the strike, not on the spot rate at the time of the exercise or at the time of the original trade. It is a common, but dangerous error to calculate the premium as a percentage of the Deutschmark amount, i.e.

DM 1,000,000 × 3% = DM 30,000.

If the spot rate is different from the strike, say DM 1.80, then calculating the premium by this method will give a totally different US dollar premium amount, i.e.

DM 30,000 ÷ DM 1.80 = $16,666.

Therefore, when premium is expressed as a percentage it means as a percentage of the US dollar amount through the strike, i.e. the US dollar amount which will be delivered upon exercise.

Example 4 expresses the premium in Deutschmarks per US dollar:

4. Buy a 5 March US dollar put (DM call) struck at DM 2.00 for DM 0.0540 (usually expressed as '5.4 pfennigs').

In examples 2 and 3 the spot $/DM rate was not mentioned, and is in fact irrelevant to the premium calculation because the terms used throughout are in US dollars. When expressed as a foreign currency per US dollar, the spot rate is, indeed, very relevant. Assuming that the spot $/DM rate is DM 1.80 the premium in example 4 is calculated by multiplying the figure by the US dollar amount:

DM 1,000,000 ÷ DM 2.00 = $500,000 (US dollar amount)
$500,000 × DM 0.0540 = DM 27,000
This is the equivalent of DM 27,000 per $500,000 or DM 27,000/$500,000 = DM 0.0540

The Deutschmark premium amount can be converted back into US dollars through the spot rate:

DM 27,000 ÷ DM 1.80 = $15,000

While active participants in the market will happily quote option premiums in any of the previously mentioned ways, and switch from one quotation style to another as easily as picking up another telephone, in order to avoid unnecessary confusion and to give some standardisation to the many examples given in this book, the reciprocal or IMM or Philadelphia style of quotation has been preferred; however, where it seems more appropriate, such as with currencies that are normally traded 'European' style in the spot market (yen, Deutschmarks etc.) the same convention has been adopted for the options. As foreign exchange markets worldwide use the same quotation style for sterling – $ per pound at all times – I have tended to favour examples based on sterling to the unavoidable exclusion of other currencies.

American and European style options

American options

The holder of an American option has the right to exercise his option at any time until expiry. The writer of an American option may be assigned at any time, and on the discretion of the buyer.

European options

The holder of a European style option has the right to exercise his option only on the expiry day. The writer of a European option may be assigned only on the expiration day of the option.

One point should be mentioned here; because the holder of a European option may only exercise on the day of expiry – he cannot exercise early, in other words – this in no way prohibits him from trading the position, buying more options or liquidating his holding, at any time he wishes. The difference between European and American option pricing will be discussed in the next chapter, as well as the reasoning behind early exercise of American options; but it is important to realise that the lack of an early exercise provision should not cause any trading disadvantages in an efficient market.

Exercise procedures

In the same fashion as with any other option market, exercise of a currency option results in the delivery of the underlying contract. The difference, of course, is that the underlying transaction is an exchange of currencies; the holder of a Swiss franc put who exercises the option will deliver Swiss francs to the writer in exchange for US dollars; the holder of a call option on Japanese yen who elects to exercise will receive Japanese yen and deliver US dollars (at a predetermined foreign exchange rate which is the strike price). Exercise procedures vary according to whether the underlying contract is traded on an organised exchange or in the OTC market; the exchanges have specific delivery mechanisms which may vary considerably and exchange brokers may themselves adapt the procedures according to the customer. On the OTC market the exercise of a currency option is exactly the same as if a spot trade had taken place.

For example, if the holder of a SF 10,000,000 call option struck at $0.625 (SF 1.60) decides to exercise he will receive SF 10,000,000 and deliver to the writer $6,250,000. The settlement of the transaction will be exactly as if a spot trade had taken place; upon receipt of the exercise notice the Swiss francs will be received and the US dollars delivered 'spot value', that is in two business days' time. It is normal procedure when trading OTC options to quote expiry and 'value date', e.g.: 'buy an STG ten million $1.60 call expiring 7 May, value 9 May'. Conventionally, although by no means a market rule, OTC options expire at 3.00 p.m. London time on the expiry day or 10.00 a.m. New York time. But of course, the OTC market being by definition a flexible market, the expiry time is a movable feast.

CHAPTER 3

Components of the option premium

Intrinsic and time value

The option premium can be split into two parts: intrinsic value and time value. Intrinsic value can be defined as the amount the option would be worth were it to be exercised immediately. In other words it is the difference, if any, between the strike and the spot. For example, with a stock, XYZ, trading at $100 per share, the $90 American-style call option has intrinsic value of $10. Another way of expressing this is to say that the $90 call option is 'in-the-money' by $10. Any option trading below intrinsic value represents a riskless profit opportunity for the arbitrageur. For example:

```
XYZ share price ................................................................. $100
Strike ............................................................................. $90
Premium ........................................... $10 (no arbitrage opportunity)
```

But if the option is trading at only $9:

```
XYZ share price ................................................................. $100
Strike ............................................................................. $90
Premium ........................................................................... $9
Buy the $90 call for $9/exercise option/simultaneously sell XYZ shares for $100
```

```
Gain on shares: $100 − $90  =  $10
Call option cost            =  $9
Net profit                  =  $1
```

Intrinsic value is simply the amount the option would be worth on expiry; a currency call option has value on expiry by the amount the spot rate is higher than the strike (see Fig. 3.1); a currency put option has value on expiry by the amount the spot rate is below the strike. An option will not be worth anything more than intrinsic value on expiry because there is no inherent advantage in owning it. Only if the option has some time remaining before expiry will it have any value in addition to its intrinsic worth; the level of additional premium depends upon the chances of the

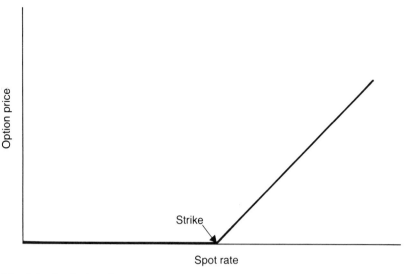

Fig. 3.1   Intrinsic value.

price moving higher by the time the option expires. The call option buyer will pay more than the intrinsic value if he feels there is a chance that the market will move above the strike by expiry; the writer will demand a premium over and above intrinsic value to cover himself against the risk of the spot moving above the strike by expiry, and therefore of the option being 'called away' from him; for this reason this extra premium is sometimes known as 'risk' premium, sometimes 'net' or 'extrinsic' premium, but more commonly 'time value'. At any time before expiry the in-the-money option premium is made up of intrinsic and time value. At-, or out-of-the-money options have strikes at or above the spot rate; these have no intrinsic value and are made up solely of time value.

The higher the spot moves above the strike (for a call option) the greater the premium. For example:

Deutschmark spot $0.55 (DM 1.8181)

	Premium =	Intrinsic value	+	Time value
$0.50 call........	$0.0530 =	$0.0500	+	$0.0030
$0.55 call........	$0.0125 =	nil	+	$0.0125
$0.60 call........	$0.0060 =	nil	+	$0.0060

Not only is the in-the-money option more expensive than the at- or out-of-the-money options but the time value element of the option decreases as the option moves further in-the-money (see Fig. 3.2). Eventually, once the option is very deep in-the-money, it loses virtually all its time value and trades only for intrinsic value. The reason is because the option will

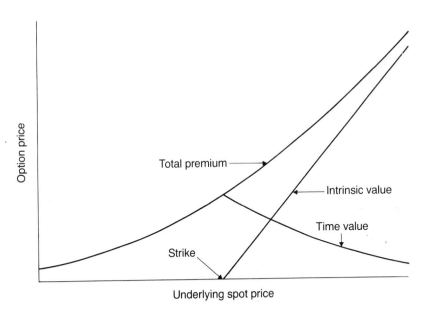

Fig. 3.2   Intrinsic and time value.

almost certainly be exercised and therefore the buyer will not pay, nor will the writer demand, any risk premium over and above intrinsic value.

The option still has value (time value only) even if the strike is above the spot (out-of-the-money); this is because the market believes that there is a chance that the spot will move higher than the strike price before the option expires. One of the reasons for this is that there is sufficient time remaining before expiry; indeed, the longer the maturity of the option the greater the premium. Obviously, an option with one year before expiry will be worth more than the same option with only one month left till expiry; the chances of larger price movements are greater for the longer-dated option and consequently the option is more likely to move in-the-money and be exercised (see Fig. 3.3).

The effect of increased time value on an option premium is not linear, however. All things being equal, an at-the-money three month option is only worth about 70 per cent more than the value of a one month option (not 300 per cent of its value); a one year option is only worth 35 per cent more than a six month option (not 200 per cent of its value). In fact, the relationship is based not on time but on the square root of time ($\sqrt{3} \div \sqrt{1} = 1.7$; $\sqrt{12} \div \sqrt{6} = 1.4$).

As a consequence, the premium for at-the-money options declines at an accelerating rate towards expiry (see Fig. 3.4). This has important implications for option traders and hedgers. Other things being equal,

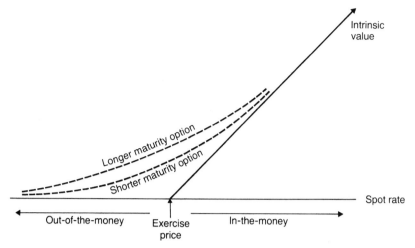

Fig. 3.3   Time to expiry.

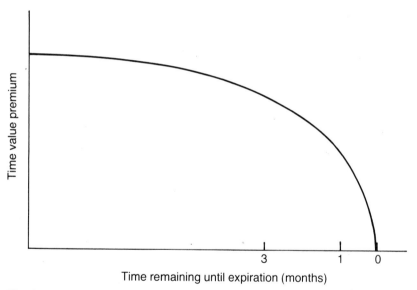

Time remaining until expiration (months)

Fig. 3.4   Time value premium decay.

short-dated options are more 'expensive', in annualised percentage terms, than options with longer maturities, and the time value of shorter-dated options declines faster over time than for longer-dated options. Hedgers, therefore, who buy options find better value for money in longer rather than shorter maturities; it is a mistake, for example, when

intending to hedge a six month time horizon to buy a three month op
with the intention of buying another three month option when
original call has expired. If the market remains unchanged the total
of the three month options combined will be higher than the original
premium cost of a six month option. Option writers, on the other hand,
usually sell shorter-dated options in order to take advantage of the
accelerating time decay.

It should be noted, however, that this effect of accelerating loss of time
value is only valid for at-the-money options. Both in-the-money and out-
of-the-money options lose premium on more of a straight line basis.
Indeed, premium decay for deep in- or out-of-the-money options may
well decelerate with the approach of expiry (see Fig. 3.5).

Volatility

The greater the chances of the underlying currency moving higher or
lower over the time period of the option, the higher will be the premium.
Currencies inside the EMS mechanism, for example, show relatively
small variations against each other. Figure 3.6 shows the Belgian franc
against the Deutschmark over a twelve month period beginning in April
1986; the maximum variation is about 3 per cent. By contrast, the

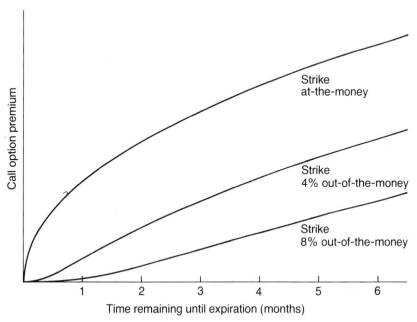

Fig. 3.5   Call option premium decay.

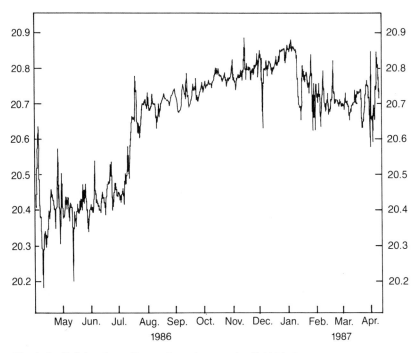

Fig. 3.6   Belgian franc/Deutschmark spot, April 1986–7.

Deutschmark/dollar chart over the same period (Fig. 3.7) shows a high/low move of over 25 per cent.[1]

Obviously, with this kind of variation the buyer of a three month Deutschmark call option struck 5 per cent out-of-the-money would be willing to pay a reasonable premium because there is a good chance that the currency will move above the strike price before expiry. The buyer of a call option on Belgian francs against Deutschmarks, however, is unlikely even to consider buying an option struck 5 per cent out-of-the-money given the lack of movement in normal circumstances; at any event he would be very unlikely to pay the same premium as for the Deutschmark/dollar option. Therefore, the more the underlying currency is expected to fluctuate, the greater will be the option premium; the buyer will be willing to pay more and the writer will want to receive more to compensate him for taking on a greater risk.

The statistical measure normally used to gauge the volatility of markets is the standard deviation, more correctly the standard deviation of daily

[1] Interestingly, were this move to be expressed in reciprocal terms the Deutschmark can be seen to have rallied from about $0.4160 to $0.5580; an increase of about 35 per cent.

Fig. 3.7   Deutschmark spot, April 1986–7.

percentage changes in the underlying price. Volatility describes the size of likely price variations, specifically of price variations around the trend rather than the trend itself. The figure is usually annualised to give a constant measure; annualised volatility of 20 per cent, for example, means that the currency has a 68 per cent chance of being up or down within a 20 per cent band within one year; consequently, there is a 32 per cent chance that the currency will have moved up or down by more than 20 per cent in one year's time. It is possible to convert this figure into a daily volatility measure by dividing the annualised figure by the square root of the number of trading days in a year ($\sqrt{250} = 15.8$). For example, with spot sterling at $1.50 and volatility at 20 per cent the probability of sterling being up or down within the range of about two cents over a one day period is 68 per cent; there is a 32 per cent chance that sterling will move more than two cents during the same period. (20 per cent annual volatility ÷ 15.8 = 1.26 per cent daily volatility. $1.50 × 1.26 per cent = $0.0189 or 1.89 cents per pound.) Volatility of 10 per cent equates to a 68 per cent probability of sterling moving inside a one cent 'confidence interval', and a 32 per cent chance of moving by more than one cent from one day to the next.

Volatility is a key variable in option pricing. For at-the-money options the relationship is linear; that is, a doubling of volatility results in a doubling of the option premium (see Fig. 3.8). Unfortunately for such a critical variable it is also the most used and abused word in the option trader's vocabulary. It would not be an exaggeration to say that it is misunderstood by a large number of professionals in the market (this does not prevent them making money, however); and yet of those who understand the concept there is no consensus about how to measure it. Unfortunately, unlike any other variable, volatility is an intangible; we can measure the intrinsic value of an option, for example, but we cannot see volatility.

Essentially there are two ways of looking at volatility. The first is to calculate the standard deviation of a given series of spot prices. This is known as historic volatility. Traders will analyse the data over 10 trading days, 30 days, 90 days, 360 days or beyond. Alternatively, given that the spot foreign exchange market is a world-wide 24-hour market, one might look at intra-day data, perhaps taking four prices per day (one every six hours). What the trader is trying to do is to find a measure of volatility which adequately explains the way the market has been moving and,

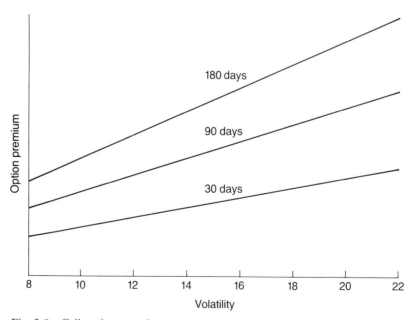

Fig. 3.8   Call option premiums.

more significantly, will give a reasonable idea of how the market is likely to move in the future. Currency market volatility is not a constant figure, unfortunately; the volatility of the Belgian franc against the Deutschmark may be very low on the basis of the last twelve months' data, but it will be little guide to future volatility if an EMS realignment is imminently anticipated; volatility for the Deutschmark/US dollar may well have been high in 1986, but in an era of more active central bank intervention, with the emphasis on stability in foreign exchange markets, this historic figure may be of academic interest only.

The second method of measuring volatility is to look at the premiums trading in the market, in Philadelphia or on the IMM for example, and to calculate the volatility figure implied by the level of the option premium. This method is thus known as 'implied volatility'. It is a matter of turning the option on its head, finding out what other traders and market-makers think volatility should be and then deciding whether or not this is an accurate representation of future volatility.

Traders often compare historic and implied volatility figures.[2] Figures

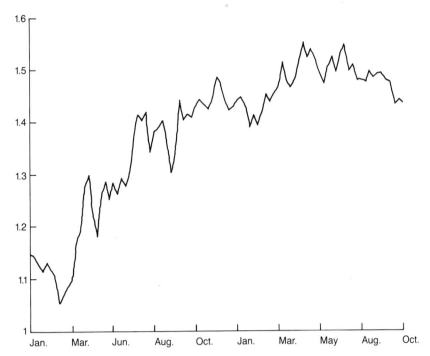

Fig. 3.9   Sterling spot, January 1985–October 1986.

[2] Volatility graphs are reproduced by permission of the currency options desk of Donaldson, Lufkin, and Jenrette International.

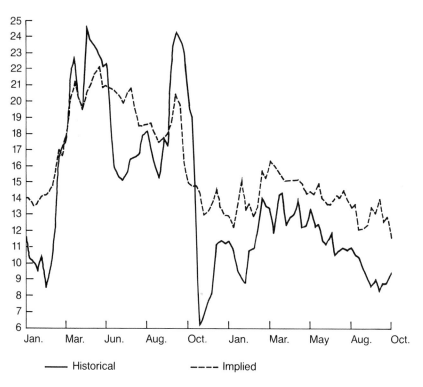

Fig. 3.10 Sterling volatility: implied versus historical, January 1985–October
1986.

3.9–3.16 compare the historic and implied volatilities for sterling, Swiss
francs, Deutschmarks and Japanese yen. The historical figure in each
case is the 30 day standard deviation; the implied figure is the one month
volatility taken from the exchanges and from the OTC market. As a
comparison the chart of the underlying market is also included. It can be
seen that the historic and implied figures have reasonable correlations but
there are significant differences between the two; sometimes the historical figure will be higher than the implied, and sometimes the opposite
effect will take place. Sometimes the historic will appear to lead, and
conversely sometimes it will appear to lag behind the implied figure.
There is no magic in these figures, no automatic route to profitability from
studying the graphs; but they do point very clearly to the reason for the
underlying uncertainty in the market-place concerning this critical variable, volatility.

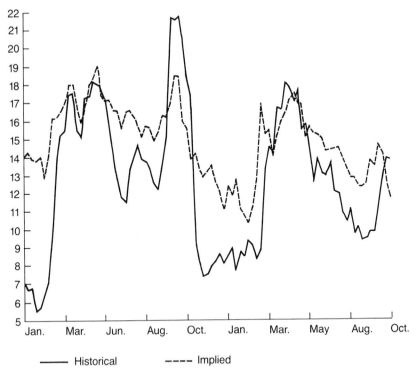

Fig. 3.11   Deutschmark spot: implied versus historical, January 1985–October 1986.

Interest rate differentials

The effect of interest rates on the option premium is the least intuitively obvious, and yet, particularly with currency options, it is one of the most important components of the premium. In stock options, the higher the interest rate, the higher the call option premium. This can be explained in the following way: assume that the investment manager puts together a portfolio comprising US Treasury bills and stock options. With the one year bill paying five per cent interest he buys $1,000,000 of bills and spends $50,000 on stock options. The resulting position is riskless; the interest from the bills will cover the cost of the options and if the stock market stays at the same level or falls over the next twelve months the options will expire worthless but the original $1 million remains secure, invested as it is in a riskless security. Discounting the effects of dividends, the performance of the T. bill/option strategy should therefore be the same as a full equity investment in a flat market. If the stock market either plunges or soars in the next twelve months the T. bill/option strategy may

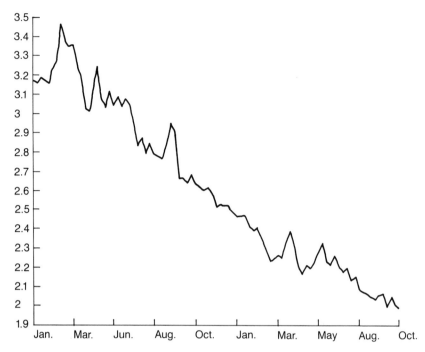

Fig. 3.12 Deutschmark volatility, January 1985–October 1986.

well outperform the strategy of being fully invested in equities; following a collapse in the stock market, the bill/option holder will at least have his investment intact, and following a strong rally the leverage inherent in the options position will allow the bill/option holder to at least match the performance of the equity investor. Therefore, should Treasury bill rates rise, say from 5 per cent to 6 per cent, the portfolio manager will have an extra $10,000 to invest in call options; hence the call option premium should correspondingly rise.

Alternatively, compare stocks with options on stocks as two leveraged instruments; because the stock market buyer has to borrow more money in order to invest in equities than if he bought call options, the cost of borrowing becomes significant. For example, if interest rates rise sharply the investor may prefer to switch out of stocks into options on stocks as a cheaper method of keeping his exposure in the market. If interest rates fall to zero, however, the investor would be able to borrow at no cost at all in order to buy stocks; he could leverage himself almost infinitely in the stock market itself and therefore would have no need to buy options. Consequently call option premiums (for equities) will rise or fall in relation to the rate of interest in the market.

In currency options the situation is complicated by the fact that there

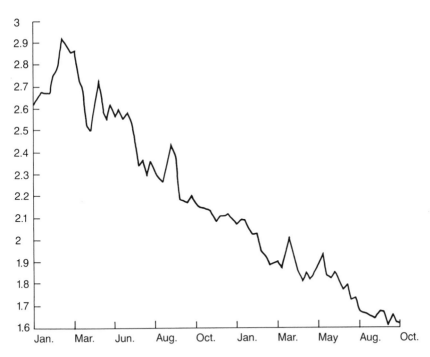

Fig. 3.13   Spot Swiss franc, January 1985–October 1986.

are two interest rates involved in foreign exchange pricing, the domestic rate (usually in US dollars) and the interest rate of the foreign currency. But the principle is the same. The premium of a currency call option will increase if the US dollar rate increases in relation to the interest rate of the foreign currency. This is because holding a foreign currency and buying a currency call option are two alternative strategies for the currency investor; on the one hand the investor will sell (borrow) US dollars and buy (invest in) the foreign currency in order to take advantage of any anticipated gains in the market; alternatively he might simply buy a currency call option. If the US dollar interest rate rises the cost of borrowing (selling) US dollars will increase which will make the currency option alternative more attractive, thus pushing up its premium.

Of course, the US dollar interest rate might remain the same but the foreign currency interest rate might fall. The effect on the interest rate differential and therefore on the call option premium will be the same; it will be less attractive to the investor to borrow in dollars and invest in the foreign currency and therefore the alternative strategy of buying a currency call option will have an advantage, hence the premium will rise.

Similarly, for put option buying, which is simply the equivalent of the right to borrow in the foreign currency, a decrease in US dollar interest

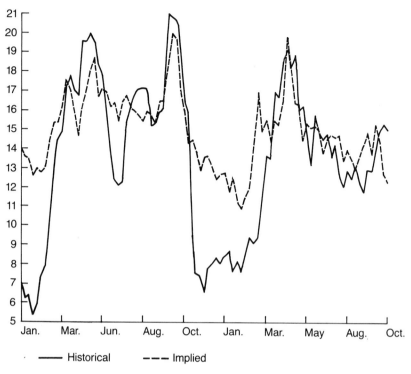

Fig. 3.14   Swiss franc volatility: implied versus historical, January 1985–October
1986.

rates or an increase in the foreign currency interest rate will make the
alternative strategy of buying currency put options more attractive, and
therefore the put premium will increase.

The effect of interest rate differential changes on currency option
premiums can be summarised as follows:

1.   Assuming the spot rate remains unchanged, a rise in US dollar
     interest rates relative to the foreign currency interest rate, or a fall in
     the foreign currency interest rate relative to the dollar interest rate,
     will increase the premium for a currency call option and decrease the
     premium for a currency put option.
2.   Assuming the spot rate remains the same, a fall in the US dollar
     interest rate relative to the foreign currency interest, or a rise in the
     foreign currency interest rate in relation to the US dollar interest
     rate, will decrease the premium for a currency call option and
     increase the premium for a currency put option.

To understand by how much this interest rate differential change will
affect the premium it is important to have an understanding of the

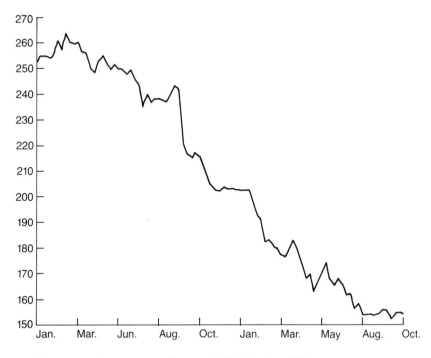

Fig. 3.15   Spot Japanese yen, January 1985–October 1986.

forward price mechanism at work in the foreign exchange market. The forward price of a currency is a function of the spot price and the interest rate differential between the two currencies, what is known as the interest rate parity. If one year US dollar interest rates are 6 per cent, and one year sterling interest rates are 10 per cent, the price of sterling one year forward must be 4 per cent below the spot; if the forward and the spot price were the same an arbitrage profit of 4 per cent would result from borrowing in dollars, investing in sterling and selling sterling one year forward.

In commodity and financial markets interest rate parity is known as the 'cost of carry' where the forward or futures price depends on the cost of borrowing money in order to hold the position. For example, with spot gold at $400 and one year interest rates at 10 per cent, the price of gold one year forward will be about $440. If it is any higher, arbitrageurs will sell the forward and buy the spot, thus locking in a return higher than the cost of borrowing money for one year. Another way of expressing this relationship is to say that the buyer of gold is indifferent to borrowing money at 10 per cent in order to hold gold for 12 months, or to paying a 10 per cent premium to the spot price in order to buy gold in one year's time.

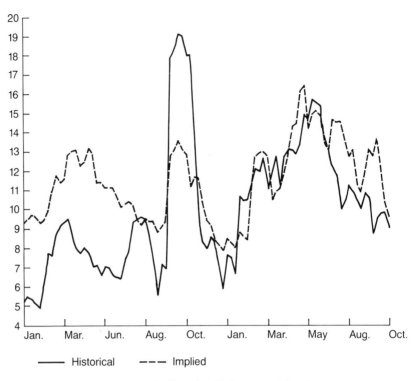

Fig. 3.16 Japanese yen volatility: implied versus historical, January 1985–
October 1986.

With securities such as bonds, which have coupon income, the forward
price depends not simply on the cost of borrowing funds but on the
difference between the cost of borrowing and the accrued interest on the
bond. In a normal yield curve, where the coupon income is greater than
the short term borrowing rate, arbitrageurs will force the forward price of
the bond below the spot by exactly the level of the interest rate differential. Thus a potential buyer will be indifferent to, say, buying a cash bond
with a current yield of 7 per cent and funding the position at 5 per cent, or
to buying the same bond in the forward market at a 2 per cent discount to
the cash price.

In exactly the same way interest rate parity or the cost of carry forces
the forward rate of sterling below the spot by exactly the amount of the
interest rate differential. Arbitrageurs will ensure that no advantage will
accrue from borrowing in dollars and investing in sterling or by buying
sterling at the forward rate. The 'swap points', the differential between a
currency's spot and forward rate, are an integral factor in assessing the
level of premium for a currency option. Just by analysing the intrinsic

value of an option in relation to the forward price of the currency both the effect of interest rate differentials and the apparent anomalies concerning American and European pricing and early exercise can be more easily understood. For example:

Spot sterling $1.50
Forward sterling $1.45

	Intrinsic value
$1.40 call American style	$0.10
$1.40 call European style	$0.05
$1.50 call American style	Nil
$1.50 call European style	Nil
$1.50 put American style	$0.05
$1.50 put European style	$0.05
$1.60 put American style	$0.15
$1.60 put European style	$0.15

It can be seen that the American in-the-money call ($1.40 strike) has more intrinsic value than the same strike European call; the at-the-money calls, both American and European style, have no intrinsic value (which is only what one would expect according to the definition of an at-the-money option). However, not only do the at-the-money puts, both American and European style, both have intrinsic value, but the level of this intrinsic value for both at- and in-the-money American and European puts is the same. Why should this be so?

Taking the calls first, the $1.40 American call must be worth at least 10 cents because anything less and an arbitrage profit would result from immediate exercise (exactly the same as with the call option example on XYZ stock). Intrinsic value for American calls, therefore, is simply the amount that the spot is greater than the strike, its in-the-money amount, in other words. But European options, by definition, cannot be exercised before the expiry date; indeed they can be defined as options on the forward price of a currency to a forward date. Where early exercise is impossible the level of spot is irrelevant. The only benchmark is the forward price, known as the forward outright.

Thus intrinsic value for the $1.40 European call is only 5 cents (forward price – strike). Similarly, the intrinsic value of the $1.50 put is 5 cents (strike – forward) and for the $1.60 put is 15 cents ($1.60 – $1.45). An arbitrage opportunity would only exist for the European call if it were possible to buy the option for a premium less than the difference between the strike and the forward outright. For example:

Buy $1.40 European call option for $0.04 (equivalent of buying sterling forward at $1.44)

Sell sterling forward at $1.45. Minimum profit on a forward date; $0.01.[3]

If European options give the right to buy or sell a currency at a forward price to a forward date, American options, by contrast, give the right to buy or sell a currency at the spot price to a forward date. Therefore, in the case of sterling puts, American style, the forward points must be included in the definition of intrinsic value in the same way as with European options. If the $1.60 European put has 15 cents intrinsic value ($1.60–$1.45) the $1.60 American put in our example must also be worth the difference between the strike and the forward (15 cents), not between the strike and the spot (10 cents). Otherwise the anomaly would exist of an American option trading at a lower premium than a European option with the same strike and maturity; this would present another simple arbitrage opportunity: thus buy the American option, sell the European option, and wait for convergence on expiration day at the latest.

Therefore, in order to create an arbitrage opportunity from an American style put on sterling it is necessary to buy the put, buy sterling forward and wait until the forward date in order to force the profit from the two legs of the arbitrage – that is in exactly the same manner as with any European style option.

In the case of currencies with lower interest rates than US dollars – normally Deutschmarks, Swiss francs, yen etc. – the intrinsic value of American and European calls and puts are the exact mirror image of higher interest rate currencies like sterling. For example:

Deutschmark spot $0.5450 (DM 1.8348)
Forward rate $0.5500

	Intrinsic value
$0.5400 American call	$0.0100
$0.5400 European call	$0.0100

---

[3] The arbitrage of a European currency option against the forward outright usually entails waiting until the convergence of the forward with the option; that is, the arbitrageur may have to wait until the expiration date of the option, so that, as with this example, he can force a profit by exercising his $1.40 call, taking delivery of sterling through the option, and simultaneously delivering his sterling to satisfy his forward sale commitment. The advantage, however, is that arbitrage of a European option with the forward establishes a minimum but not a maximum profit. For example:

Sterling spot on expiration day: $1.10
Call is abandoned – cost: $0.04
Profit on forward trade: $0.35 ($1.45–$1.10)
Net profit: $0.31

Such a trade buying a call/selling the currency forward is an example of a 'synthetic put' because it has the same profit or loss exposure as a long put option. (See the following chapter for a review of 'synthetics'.)

| $0.5600 American put | $0.0150 |
| $0.5600 European put | $0.0100 |

Here, the in-the-money calls have the same intrinsic value because there is no advantage in exercising early; the only arbitrage opportunity available is through holding the call option until expiry. The puts, however, have higher intrinsic value for American than for European options; the American $0.56 put option, if exercised immediately, is worth 150 points; the European put option, being an option on the forward price to a forward date, is worth only the difference between the strike and the forward ($0.5600–$0.5500 = $0.0100 or 100 points). For currency options, therefore, the standard definition of intrinsic value as used with equity options will not suffice. Intrinsic value for currency options can be defined as follows:

1. For European style options the premium must be at least the difference between the strike and the forward foreign exchange rate.[4]
2. For American style options the premium must be at least the difference between the strike and the forward foreign exchange rate, or between the strike and the spot rate, whichever is the greater.

We know that, as a consequence of these definitions, sterling calls, American style, are more expensive than sterling calls European style; this is because the European option is only arbitrageable against the forward whereas the American option can be traded against the benchmark of the spot rate. Puts on sterling, by contrast, are the same whether American or European because the difference between the strike and the forward (the definition of a European option) is greater than the difference between the strike and the spot rate (and we know that a European option cannot be more expensive than an American option). The implication of these relationships can be summarised as follows. Given the same strikes and maturities:

1. For currencies with higher interest rates than US dollars (normally sterling, lira, Australian dollars etc.) American call options have a higher premium than European call options. American and European puts have the same value.
2. For currencies with lower interest rates than US dollars (normally Deutschmarks, Swiss francs, yen, etc.) American and European call options have the same premium, American puts have a higher premium than European puts.
3. Only in the case of a currency having the identical interest rate as US dollars will the premium for calls and puts, American and European be the same.

---

[4] Strictly speaking, the difference between the spot and forward foreign exchange rates should be discounted to present value.

In the equity option market an at-the-money option is, by definition, struck at the same price as the stock. With currency options, however, a put struck at the spot rate on a higher interest rate currency like sterling or a call struck at the spot rate on a lower interest rate currency like Deutschmarks, is in-the-money versus the forward. In other words, because the forward points may be included in the option premium the definition of an at-the-money currency option has to be rephrased:

1. A call option on a higher interest rate currency struck at the spot is at-the-money. A put on a higher interest rate currency struck at the spot is in-the-money versus the forward foreign exchange rate. By convention, therefore, an at-the-money put is struck at the forward rate.
2. A call option on a lower interest rate currency struck at the spot is in-the-money versus the forward foreign rate. By convention, therefore, an at-the-money call is struck at the forward rate. At-the-money puts are struck at the spot.

For example, at-the-money calls on sterling, lira, Australian dollars etc. (normally higher interest rate currencies), are struck at the spot, but puts are conventionally struck at the forward because puts struck at the spot have intrinsic value by the amount of interest rate differentials. By contrast at-the-money calls on Deutschmarks, Swiss francs, yen etc. (normally lower interest rate currencies), are by convention struck at the forward outright because calls struck at the spot have intrinsic value by the amount of the forward points (interest rate differential). At-the-money puts are struck at the spot rate.

American options: the value of the early exercise provision

It can be seen from the previous series of definitions that the relative value of European and American options is simply a function of arbitrage relationships between the spot rate and the interest rates of the two currencies. For example, in normal circumstances call options on Deutschmarks are the same whether they are American or European. American puts on Deutschmarks, on the other hand, trade at a higher premium than European puts. No added value is given for the fact that American options are exercisable at any time; no discount is allowed for European options in spite of the possible inconvenience of only being able to exercise on the expiration day. This begs the question of whether the flexibility of an American option is worth anything extra over and above its theoretical premium. To put it another way, if a sterling put has the same premium American or European style, is there any reason not to prefer the American option? Alternatively, if a European call on sterling is always cheaper than the equivalent American call (as long as sterling interest rates are higher than dollar rates), is there any advantage in paying more for an American style option?

In practice, and for most circumstances, there is very little extra advantage. Take, for example, the holder of an American style $1.50 call on sterling expiring in six months' time. If the holder needs to take delivery of sterling before the expiration date he has the choice of exercising the call option early, which, by definition, means he buys sterling at the spot rate of $1.50, or alternatively, he can sell the option for at least its intrinsic value, and buy sterling at the current spot rate in the market. But selling, rather than exercising the option, is never the worst strategy, and is often the best alternative. If the option has any residual time value left this will certainly be the case:

Spot sterling $1.60
$1.50 call option bid 11 cents
(A) Exercise option: Equivalent of buying sterling at $1.50

(B) Sell option for 11 cents/
Buy spot at $1.60:   Equivalent of buying sterling at $1.49
                        ($1.60–$0.11)

As long as an option has any time value remaining it should never be exercised early; the only occasion when an American option must be exercised rather than sold is when it is trading for less than intrinsic value, that is when the market itself is inefficient. The exercise of the option forces convergence with the spot rate, for example:

	Optimum strategy
Spot sterling $1.60	
(A) $1.50 call bid 9 cents (below intrinsic)	Exercise option
(B) $1.50 call bid 10 cents (intrinsic value)	Either (a) Exercise option, or (b) Sell option and buy spot
(C) $150 call bid 11 cents (1 cent above intrinsic)	Sell option and buy spot

Under normal circumstances, of course, the market should be efficient, and therefore the option should always be worth at least its intrinsic value; consequently only alternatives B or C should be applicable. For the holder of a European option there is no opportunity, by definition, to exercise early. However, given an efficient market we have already shown that the early exercise provision is of little significant added value. The European option can be sold for its intrinsic value (at least) and spot currency purchased. There are two possible disadvantages to this strategy, however. One, because the intrinsic value of a European option is only the difference between the strike and the forward rate, not between the strike and the spot rate, the intrinsic value of a European sterling call option will be less than its American style counterpart by the amount of the forward points. There is a penalty, therefore, for buying a European call option. But the closer to the expiration date the smaller will be the effect of the interest rate differential on the forward points and the smaller will be the penalty for taking the currency early. For example, looking at a transaction from beginning to end:

1 March: spot sterling $1.50. 1 October forward $1.4675.

American style $1.50 1 October call: 5 cents
European style $1.50 1 October call: 4.7 cents

1 April: spot sterling $1.75. 1 October forward rate $1.7150

American style $1.50 1 October call: 25 cents
European style $1.50 1 October call: 21.5 cents

1 September: Spot sterling $1.75. 1 October forward rate $1.7430

American style $1.50 1 October call: 25 cents
European style $1.50 1 October call: 24.3 cents

It can be seen that the buyer of a currency option who intends to take delivery but who does not know the precise date on which he may need the currency – which is often the case with many hedgers – may have to weigh up the advantage of buying a cheaper European option with the risk of paying a penalty for selling it early. The earlier the transaction is closed out the greater the potential penalty. On 1 March, the holder of the European option received 3.5 cents less than if he had purchased an American call and had been able to exercise early; this was because sterling rallied so sharply and the option became so deep in-the-money. Indeed, he might well have decided that the risks of sterling rallying 25 cents within one month were too slight to be a serious risk.

Furthermore, a change in interest rate differential can also affect the premium, advantageously or otherwise. A sharp increase in differentials by 1 March, for example, would have resulted in a much greater forward discount for sterling, and a greater penalty for the holder of the European option. A narrowing of the differentials, by contrast, would reduce this penalty or in some circumstances eliminate it altogether. In conclusion it is more a question of judgement than of mathematics.

The other potential disadvantage in buying a European rather than an American style option depends on the option user's familiarity or lack of it with the foreign exchange market itself. Some buyers of currency options are by no means professional traders in foreign exchange; many smaller companies have never used the forward market, either because of inexperience or because their credit status is insufficient to allow them the facility to trade forward on an unsecured basis, i.e. their banks will not give them a line. For some the only use they make of the spot market is to contact their bank on an infrequent basis in order to buy or sell relatively small amounts of foreign currency. They are certainly not in a position, unlike professional traders, to check spot prices or to monitor the market closely. Sometimes, even for professionals, the precise level of spot, and therefore the intrinsic value of the option, can be a matter of debate; this is particularly likely in the case of thinly traded 'exotic' or cross-rate currency, or when the market generally is trading erratically, such as during a period of central bank intervention or following the release of a surprise piece of economic or political news. In such circumstances it might be more convenient to buy an American option and exercise when the currency is needed rather than pay marginally less for a European option and incur extra transaction costs in selling the option and buying spot. If the amounts are small the spreads in the spot market may well be wide and the overall costs will increase. Of course, for those with currency hedging requirements without proper access to the forward foreign exchange market, the strategy of buying options becomes very attractive because for the cost of the premium the buyer has hedged himself and still has an opportunity to profit if the currency moves in his direction. The corollary of this situation is the option writer who sells a European rather than an American option because he is willing to forgo a limited amount of premium in return for the security of knowing that the option will not be assigned when he least expects it. This begs the question: why is a currency option likely to be exercised early?

American options: why exercise early?

Generally, if the market is efficient, there are two reasons why an option will be exercised early. One is because the holder requires the currency before the exercise date and will save on transaction costs (for the reasons, see above); secondly an option will be exercised early if the holder loses money or sacrifices a profit by continuing to carry the option position. For example, the holder of a deep in-the-money call on a stock with the dividend due to be paid shortly may well exercise the option if the likely dividend payment is not included in the option's intrinsic value. The stock price will fall by the amount of the dividend paid as soon as the stock trades ex-dividend. The owner of the stock will receive the dividend, but the owner of the call option on the stock will not. Therefore, in order to capture the dividend payment, the owner of the option should exercise. In currencies the interest rate differential is the equivalent of a continuously-paid dividend on a stock. The difference, of course, is that the 'dividend' on a currency can be positive or negative depending on whether the interest rate of the currency is higher or lower than that of the domestic currency. Buying a call option on a currency is the alternative strategy to investing in that currency.

With higher yielding currencies such as sterling, buying a three month call option has to be compared with the strategy of selling dollars for sterling and buying a three month (higher yielding) sterling time deposit. As long as the option has time as well as intrinsic value it will probably not pay the holder to exercise early; the value of the premium, intrinsic and time value, is worth more to the holder than the higher yield on the sterling deposit. But when the option moves deep in-the-money and trades only for its intrinsic value, the holder is sacrificing real profits by continuing to keep the option and not exercising it. In similar fashion to the stock option example, the in-the-money sterling call option is simply worth its intrinsic value; he is losing the yield advantage inherent in holding the currency by continuing to hold the option, therefore he should exercise.

The optimum moment to exercise is when the time value of the option is less than the yield pick-up in the currency; that is when the time value is less than the forward points. The owner of a sterling put, by contrast, has the right to sell (borrow in) a higher yielding currency than US dollars; there is no advantage for him to exercise early in any circumstances, therefore, because by so doing he is paying unnecessary 'points away'. Similarly, the owner of a call option on a lower yielding currency like Deutschmarks should never exercise early because he is effectively investing at a lower rate than would be available through US dollars. The owner of a Deutschmark put option, however, is in the same position as the holder of a sterling call; exercise of a Deutschmark put results in the delivery (borrowing of) a lower interest rate currency; again, once the option moves deep in-the-money and loses its time value, early exercise of a Deutschmark put is advantageous over the alternative strategy of continuing to borrow in more expensive dollars. (This is another confirmation of the fact that, for example, sterling calls American style trade at a higher premium than European options, but that puts are the same, whether American or European. It is a potential advantage to own an American call option because of the possibility of investing in a higher yielding currency; there is no advantage in owning an American over a European put, however, because early exercise – meaning exercising the right to borrow at a higher rate – will inevitably result in a loss.)[5]

---

[5] One exception to this general rule is where interest rate differentials are likely to change from a premium to a discount, such as with ECUs or, occasionally, sterling itself. It may, for example, be advantageous for a buyer of sterling put options to pay more for an American than for a European style option if he feels that sterling interest rates are likely to fall below US dollar rates during the life of the option.

Another way of expressing the effect of interest rate differentials on the likelihood of early exercise is to use the commodity term of 'cost of carry'. The forward price of a currency is not in any real sense a predictor of future price movements – at best it has a poor success rate – but it is the 'best guess' of where the spot will trade at on the forward date. With sterling the cost of carry is negative because the forward price is at a discount to the spot; the spot is expected to fall to the level of the forward outright by the forward date. Therefore the holder of a deep in-the-money call on sterling should exercise early otherwise the value of his call will only reduce in value as time passes. The holder of a put option, however, should not exercise early because the premium will hold its value as the spot rate declines to meet the theoretical forward. (This argument may seem over-academic, yet it is only another way of expressing how the premiums of calls and puts are arrived at. Anyone who disputes the forward pricing theory of currencies, who does not accept, in other words, that the forward price is indeed the best guess of future price movements, has several trading opportunities open to him. These will be discussed in later chapters.)

Failure to exercise early is a real loss to the option owner or, alternatively, gives windfall profits to the option writer. The writer of a sterling call is committed to delivering a higher interest rate currency than US dollars, in other words to borrowing at a higher rate; the writer of a Deutschmark put is committed to receiving a lower interest rate currency than US dollars, in other words to investing at a lower rate; without early exercise when the sterling call or the Deutschmark put moves deep in-the-money the writer is given a free ride. Similarly, the early exercise of a sterling put or of a Deutschmark call hands over windfall profits to the writer; exercise of a sterling put gives a higher yielding currency to the option writer; exercise of a Deutschmark call enables the writer to deliver (borrow) a lower interest rate currency. In each case early exercise is a loss to the option holder.

However, there is one situation where early exercise may be possible for both calls and puts of any currency, higher or lower yielding. On the IMM in Chicago, currency futures traders are marked to the market every day. This means that they receive or pay profits or losses on their positions daily. The option buyer, however, pays the full premium 'up front' but, as with the majority of options markets around the world, he only realises a profit when he liquidates his position. Consequently, the holder of an in-the-money option on currency futures (or any other futures option for that matter), may well decide to exercise early in order to release funds which would be available to him in the form of variation margin. The optimum moment to exercise is when the interest received from investing the released variation margin is greater than the cost of carry. (The fact that many in-the-money futures options are not in fact exercised early presumably points to the continued existence of imperfections in the options markets.) Options on currency futures trade differently from other options markets due to this variation margin effect. At- or out-of-the-money options are priced like European options; this is what one would anticipate given that they are options on the forward (futures) to a forward date. But the further in-the-money the futures option moves, the more important will be this variation margin factor, and the more it will trade like an American style option. It was in order to avoid the asymmetry in the traded options market, where the buyers pay the full premium and the writers are margined, that prompted the LIFFE exchange to margin both longs and shorts, the buyers as well as the writers. This reduces or even eliminates the need to exercise in-the-money options because the holder receives credit margin from the Clearing House just as with a futures position.

The early exercise provision for currency options can be summarised as follows:

1. American call options on higher interest rate currencies or put options on lower interest rate currencies have optimum early exercise.
2. American put options on higher interest rate currencies or call options on lower interest rate currencies should not be exercised early.

CHAPTER 4

Option pricing theory

The Black–Scholes model

In 1972, not long after the start of stock options trading on the Chicago Board Options Exchange (CBOE), professors Myron Scholes and Fischer Black devised a method of calculating the fair premium for a European style call option. The methodology was explained on the first page of their published article, 'The Pricing of Options and Corporate Liabilities'.[1]

'If options are correctly priced in the market, it should not be possible to make sure profits by creating portfolios of long and short positions in options and their underlying stocks. Using this principle a theoretical valuation formula for options is derived . . . The value of the options will depend only on the price of the stock and time and on variables that are taken to be known constants. Thus it is possible to create a hedged position, consisting of a long position in the stock and a short position in the option, whose value will not depend on the price of the stock, but will depend only on time and the values of known constants . . . Thus the risk in the hedged position is zero if the short position in the option is adjusted continuously.'

Essentially the principal of the Black–Scholes pricing model is that the stock, and the call option on the underlying stock, are two comparable investments; it should be possible to create a riskless portfolio, therefore, by buying the stock and hedging it by selling the option. If the stock moves higher, so will the option, but not necessarily by the same amount. Thus it is necessary to hold only enough stock to replicate the movement of the option. By continuously adjusting the amount of stock held throughout the life of the option the position should be riskless; the income received from investing the call premium will be exactly offset by the cost of replicating (hedging) in the underlying stock market.

Figure 4.1 shows how Black and Scholes used the same variables as were described in the previous chapter to construct their fair value model.

[1] *Journal of Political Economy*, May 1972.

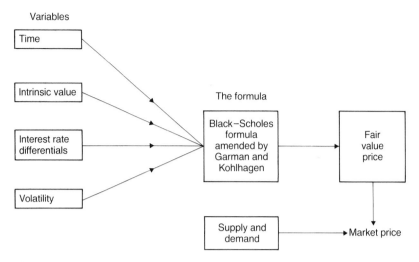

Fig. 4.1   How a currency option is priced.

What is interesting, however, is not the variables that were used in the model, but those that were left out. More particularly, it is important to note that in all this analysis to date no mention has been made of market direction or bias as an appropriate input for the model. Indeed, an assumption of the model is that the market moves in a random fashion, that while prices will change, the chances of a rise are the same as the chances of a fall, and that the likelihood of large movements relative to small movements is 'normal'. There are no gaps. It is as though one could draw a graph of the market without taking the pencil from the paper. Plotting such daily market movements over time results in the bell-shaped curve which statisticians call a 'normal distribution'. In fact, the curve is slightly skewed, or 'log-normal' (see Fig. 4.2), because while stock market prices can in theory rise without limit, they cannot fall below zero.

While the Black–Scholes model adequately explains the option premium for a European call on equities, Garman and Kohlhagen, in 1982, extended the formula to cover currency options and to allow for the fact that currency pricing involves two interest rates, not one, and that a currency can trade at a premium or discount forward depending upon the interest rate differential. In 1979, Cox, Ross and Rubinstein published a pricing model which could account for the early exercise provisions of American style options. Using the same parameters as Black and Scholes, they adopted what is known as a 'binomial' method to evaluate

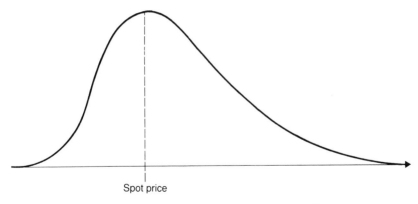

Spot price

Fig. 4.2   Log-normal distribution.

the call premium. This same binomial model is now used alongside the Garman/Kolhagen version of Black and Scholes to evaluate currency options. Assuming that early exercise will only take place if the advantage of holding the currency is greater than the time value of the option (see the explanation of early exercise for currency options in the previous chapter), the binomial method involves taking a series of trial estimates over the life of the option, each estimate being a probability analysis of early exercise for each successive day. Thus for a one year option the probability of a rise or fall in the currency is estimated for each of the 360 days until expiry; the theoretical premium for the option given various probabilities over time is compared to the cost of holding the cash hedge position; once the time value of the option is worth less than the forward points of the currency hedge the position becomes too expensive to carry and the option should be exercised. In practice, the computation of 360 'trials' would take too long, even for most computers; therefore most binomial pricing models reduce the number of trials or 'iterations' to a compromise level where the calculation process is reasonably fast and the approximation is not too great.

As we discussed in the previous chapter, the early exercise provision in American options can make a significant difference to the premium value of some options, namely calls on higher interest rate currencies and puts on lower interest rate currencies. When early exercise is unlikely, however, as with sterling puts or Swiss franc calls, the Black–Scholes and the binomial models will give identical results.

There is a danger, however, in taking the premium derived from the option pricing model, whether Black–Scholes or Cox–Ross–Rubinstein, too literally. The market price and the fair value price may well differ considerably, and while it is always possible for an arbitrageur to sell what he believes to be an overpriced option, or to buy an option which is underpriced compared to the theoretical value according to his pricing model, this will not necessarily guarantee profits. The main reason, of course, is that the inputs to his model – the underlying spot price, or the volatility, or the interest rate differentials – may vary from the rather idealised assumptions about market behaviour which Black and Scholes adopted in order to simplify the calculation process. Some of these assumptions are as follows:

1. Known (and constant) volatility.
2. Constant interest rates.
3. No transaction costs or taxation effects.
4. Continuous trading.
5. No dividends.
6. No early exercise.

Interest rate differentials will vary, of course, and sometimes errati- cally; the foreign exchange market, while the most liquid of any market in the world, does have transaction costs in the bid/ask spread, and when conditions become thin or volatile the spreads will widen and the market will gap. But while most of these assumptions are not critical to option pricing, and can either be relaxed with little effect on the premium calculation or amended (as did Cox–Ross–Rubinstein with the 'no early exercise' provision) there remain significant doubts about the underlying premises of the model. In particular, the concept of a normal or log- normal distribution is questionable as far as the foreign exchange markets are concerned. Even though foreign exchange trading, with its vast size and 24-hour basis, is the nearest imaginable to a perfect market, there are many occasions when prices do not behave in a normally distributed fashion. Wars, central bank intervention, and unexpected political or economic news are all factors which disrupt the day-to-day business of the market. Central banks and governments, for example, have a much greater regard for what happens to their own currency than they would for the price of an individual stock; governments will meet together either to agree to try and stabilise or to change foreign exchange rates, and will act in concert on occasion to influence the market.

Some currencies, formally or otherwise, are pegged to each other; the EMS, for example, is a mechanism which has worked relatively success- fully to stabilise foreign exchange rates. Similarly, until recently at least, currencies of the newly industrialised nations such as South Korea, Hong Kong, and Taiwan, as well as the currencies of some well-established industrial powers, like Canada, moved closely in tandem with the US dollar. When such currencies move out of line with this relationship it is often through political rather than market forces. Even currencies like the yen and sterling against the dollar have a tendency to move sideways for long periods followed by sharp, erratic jumps. None of these relationships could be included under the umbrella of a log-normal distribution.

Another problem which effects the currency option markets in particular is the relationship between the spot and the forward price. The forward price of a currency is its 'best guess value' at a future date; it is calculated through a eurodeposit arbitrage technique which allows banks to view all forward currency transactions as synthetic deposits. In other words a bank should be indifferent to buying another currency for delivery at a forward date, or to buying that currency in the spot market and investing in a deposit for the same date. By implication, the forward price of a currency is valid to the extent that interest rates are a reflection of inflation rates – that the higher the relative rate of inflation the higher will be the relative eurodeposit rate and the lower will be the forward price of that currency. Whether such an extension of purchasing power parity theory is indeed valid will be discussed again later, but there are some circumstances where the forward price of a currency is most unlikely to represent this best guess value. EMS currencies before a realignment, for example, can undergo large scale changes in interest rate differentials which will throw up temporary distortions in the forward price. On other occasions, as with our earlier example of Belgian francs against the Deutschmark, interest rate differentials, even in normal circumstances, can imply that the forward price of the currency is close to or even below EMS intervention support levels. There is no guarantee, of course, that the Belgian franc will not be devalued against the Deutschmark; what we do know, however, is that a mechanism exists in order to try to prevent such an eventuality. Indeed, with any currency linked directly or otherwise with another, theoretical forward premiums or discounts based on interest rate differentials may be a shaky peg on which to hang an option pricing theory.

In the real world the option pricing model works adequately for most currencies against the US dollar on a daily basis; in the longer term, the market distribution differs from the theoretical in that the chances are increased of foreign exchange rates moving higher or lower than would be implied by the log-normal distribution. This is another way of saying that the option pricing model tends to underprice out-of-the-money currency options. In the early days of the option market, banks lost money by holding religiously to the theoretical price in their models; they sold out-of-the-money options too cheaply. Nowadays, market-makers use their models as guides but tend to superimpose their own view of the market, of volatility, or of interest rates, over that of the theoretical.

Some derivatives of the option pricing model

The hedge ratio (delta)

Returning to the portfolio strategy which is the essence of option pricing theory, a call is written on the underlying currency and sufficient currency is purchased to hedge the option position. The amount of the hedge required is not static; it depends on the various inputs of the model, the level of intrinsic value, the time remaining to expiry, the interest rate differential, and the volatility of the currency itself. The greater the intrinsic value, for example, the more likely the option is to be exercised and therefore the greater the amount of currency required to hedge the option. As the currency moves higher and the option moves deeper in-the-money, an increasing amount of currency is required to hedge the position. Eventually, when the option is very deep-in-the-money, the currency should be held in a ratio of 100 per cent of the short option position. Conversely, as the underlying price falls and the option moves from very deep in-the-money to very far out-of-the-money, the ratio of the currency needed to be held as a hedge declines from 100 per cent eventually to zero.

The hedge ratio, or the delta, is the amount that should be held in the currency in order to hedge the option position. It is the rate of change in the premium given a change in the underlying currency (see Fig. 4.3).

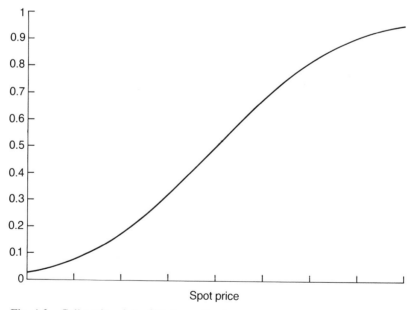

Fig. 4.3   Call option delta (30-day option).

For example, a call option on sterling struck at $1.60 costs 3 cents and has a delta of 0.4; an instantaneous move of 1 cent in the spot rate will result in an immediate increase or decrease in the option premium of 0.4 cents, i.e. with the spot at $1.61 the premium will increase to 3.4 cents, and with the spot at $1.59 the premium will fall to 2.6 cents. With a delta of 1, which would only apply to very deep in-the-money options, a 1 cent move in the spot would result in a 1 cent move in the premium. With a delta of 0.1 (for far out-of-the-money options), a 1 cent move in the spot would see the premium change by only 0.1 cents. For example:

Call (delta)		Spot rate	
$1.50 (0.9)		$1.60	$1.61
	Premium:	11 cents	11.9 cents
$1.60 (0.5)		$1.60	$1.61
	Premium:	4 cents	4.5 cents
$1.70 (0.1)		$1.60	$1.61
	Premium:	1 cent	1.1 cents

Delta can never be below zero and never, in normal circumstances, above 1; that is, an option can move one for one with the underlying currency but, all things being equal, never more than the move in the spot rate. Whereas delta for an at-the-money option is always about 0.5 the delta for out- or in-the-money options varies according to the intrinsic value of the option, the time left to expiry, the volatility of the underlying currency, and even according to the level of interest rate differentials. Indeed another way of using delta is as a probability measure; the higher the delta the greater the probability of the option being exercised. Delta is important for option traders because it provides a key to the leverage of the option position. Traders who buy far out-of-the-money options because they appear 'cheap' are often disappointed when the anticipated move in the spot market occurs and the option itself hardly moves.[2] For their part option writers should be aware of the increasing sensitivity of their short positions as the delta picks up from 0.25 through 0.35 and eventually moves above 0.5.

The gamma

The delta, the first derivative of the option pricing model, is a dynamic concept; it changes as the market changes. The gamma (the second

[2] However, while low delta options move less in absolute terms the percentage changes in the premium, as can be seen from the above examples, are very comparable. Indeed, short-dated out-of-the-money options (low delta) are likely to move more in percentage terms (but not in absolute terms) than at-the-money options. In reality, however, the effect is usually lost in the bid/ask spread which, for low premium options, is always relatively wide.

derivative of the model), describes the change in the delta given a change in the underlying price. Gamma measures the sensitivity of the delta (it is the 'delta of the delta'). The higher the gamma the higher the delta sensitivity. Gamma is at its highest for short-dated at-the-money options. This can be explained using the following exaggerated example.

If the spot sterling rate is at $1.51, the $1.50 sterling call expiring in five minutes' time has a delta of 1. In a statistical sense the option will certainly be exercised, which means that the option writer should hold 100 per cent of the currency as a hedge against his short options position. However, if the spot rate suddenly falls to $1.49 the option delta falls to zero because the option, statistically, now has a zero chance of being exercised. Therefore, no hedge is required. By contrast, consider a one year at-the-money call on sterling which has a delta of 0.47; an instantaneous move up or down in the spot rate of one cent will result in the delta moving up to 0.49 or down to 0.45 respectively. Thus:

At-the-money call deltas

Expiry	5 minutes	one year
Delta	0.5	0.47
Result of one cent increase in spot rate		
Delta	1	0.49
Result of one cent decrease in spot rate		
Delta	0	0.45

Option buyers are attracted to high gamma options because of the inherent leverage in such a position. By contrast, writers of high gamma options are taking considerable risks because of the large potential fluctuations in the premium caused by relatively small movements in the spot rate. Figure 4.4 is an illustration of gamma risk for options of different maturities and intrinsic values. A gamma of 0.1 suggests that a move of one per cent in the spot rate will result in a 0.1 move in the delta, from 0.5 to 0.6, for example.

The theta

The trade-off of high delta sensitivity (gamma) is high time decay; short-dated, at-the-money options are highly leveraged but at the same time subject to sharp premium loss in stable conditions. Low gamma options, such as longer-dated options, are less sensitive to market movement and, at the same time, experience only minor losses in premium on a day-to-day basis. The technical term for the rate of time decay is theta (see Fig. 4.5). A theta of 0.01 means that the premium will decline by 0.01 over a

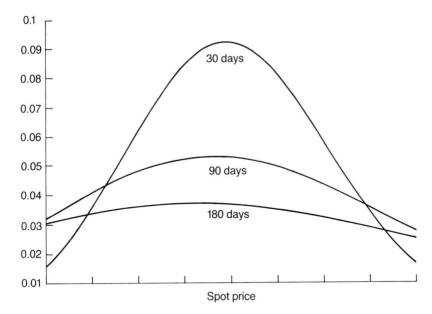

Fig. 4.4   Call option gammas.

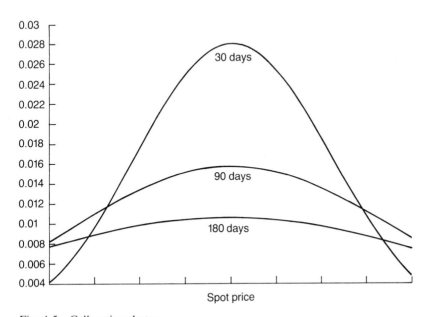

Fig. 4.5   Call option thetas.

one day period, all other factors remaining the same. It is no coincidence that the theta and gamma charts are very similar; high gamma and high theta options go hand in hand with each other. For example, to return to our sterling option expiring in five minutes, if the strike is at-the-money the delta is about 0.5 and the option is worth only time value; in five minutes' time, that is on the expiry of the option, the premium will be zero assuming the spot rate is at the same level. This is an extreme example of high time decay loss, or high theta. We also know that such an option has a very high gamma. By contrast, a very long-dated option has very little gamma or theta risk; the delta hardly changes even given comparatively large spot movements and, day-to-day, the time decay loss on the premium is virtually nil.

The vega

However, if long-dated options are insensitive to spot or time decay effects, they are very vulnerable to shifts in volatility; vega (see Fig. 4.6) is the technical term used to describe the effect on the premium of a change in volatility. A vega of 0.1 means that the premium will change by 0.1 per cent given a 1 per cent change in volatility. Whereas the time decay effect (theta) and the change in the delta (gamma) are low for long-dated

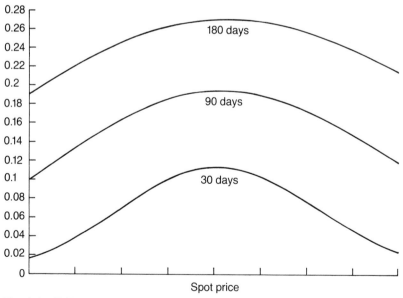

Fig. 4.6   Call option vegas.

options, the volatility sensitivity (vega) is at its highest. Again, this is another example of the trade-off effect in option markets; the currency trader may well decide to buy options rather than spot because his view of the market is that a substantial move is likely, but over a longer rather than a shorter duration. In any case he feels that, because implied volatility is at a relatively high level, the shorter-dated options are too expensive; that is, he is well aware of the possibility of high time decay loss (the high theta effect) in shorter maturity options. Consequently, he buys a one year sterling at-the-money call option. Unfortunately, in high volatility conditions, buying long-dated options may result in larger than expected losses, not through time decay loss, which is negligible day-to-day, but because of the option's sensitivity to declines in implied volatility (vega). For example:

	Expiry	Volatility	Premium
At-the-money call	1 month	15%	2.5 cents
At-the-money call	1 month	12.5%	2.0 cents
At-the-money call	12 months	15%	7.6 cents
At-the-money call	12 months	12.5%	6.1 cents

However, although the absolute loss through a fall in volatility is much higher with the longer-dated option (1.5 cents versus only a 0.5 cent loss for the one month option) the percentage fall in the one month option premium is actually slightly greater (20 per cent against 19.7 per cent). Indeed the shorter and further out-of-the-money the option, the more pronounced is this effect. For instance, using the same examples but with a $1.65 sterling call option (5 cents out-of-the-money):

Expiry	Volatility	Premium
1 month	15%	0.9 cents
1 month	12.5%	0.5 cents
12 months	15%	5.8 cents
12 months	12.5%	4.4 cents

Here, once again, the absolute loss is much larger for the twelve month than for the one month option (1.4 cents against 0.4 cents); but the percentage loss is only 24 per cent, versus a 44 per cent decline in premium for the one month option. The percentage loss due to a decline in volatility is known as vega elasticity; it is often a good corrective to see the change expressed in percentage rather than in absolute terms, particularly for the option writer who may wish to sell high vega options because he anticipates a fall in implied volatility; he will stand to make more dollars and cents by writing a long-dated, at-the-money (high vega) option, but he will make more in percentage terms by writing out-of-the-money short-dated options.

A warning about the Greek alphabet

Theta, gamma, vega, and delta are some of the checks and balances which form an integral part of the structure of the option market. Like the option pricing model itself, an understanding of their effects will not necessarily make money for the trader but, hopefully, they will prevent him from making an obviously wrong decision. They are concepts open to abuse, however. Nowadays there seems to be an over-reliance on the more esoteric side of the option business (matched by a profusion of Greek letter definitions). While it is very useful to gain a greater understanding of the intricacies of the market, it is not essential to speak Greek in order to make money out of currency options.

Currency put option pricing

Put-call parity

All option pricing models have been derived to explain the premium of call options; the value of put options can be calculated through an arbitrage process linking the call premium and the forward outright price of the currency. This is known as put-call parity.

For example, if forward sterling is at $1.60 the following relationships will apply (European options):[3]

$1.60 call	=	4 cents
$1.60 put	=	4 cents
$1.55 call	=	7 cents
$1.55 put	=	2 cents
$1.65 call	=	2 cents
$1.65 put	=	7 cents

Suppose one were to buy a $1.60 put for 4 cents and write a $1.60 call for 4 cents; the resulting cash flow is nil. If sterling rallies 5 cents the profit or loss is as follows:

Sterling $1.65	Profit or loss (cents)
Long sterling $1.60 put	0
Short sterling $0.60 call	−5
Net P&L	−5

The result is the equivalent of selling sterling short at $1.60. Selling a call and buying a put option with the same strikes is indeed the same as selling the currency short; specifically, selling a European call and buying a

---

[3] For the sake of simplicity, no allowance has been made for present valuation in any of the given examples.

European put option is identical to selling the currency at the strike rate. It is known as a synthetic short.

Were sterling in the forward market to be trading at $1.59 it would be possible to establish an arbitrage profit. Thus:

Buy sterling forward at $1.59
Sell $1.60 call for 4 cents
Buy $1.60 put for 4 cents.

This trade, known as a forward conversion, will lock in a 1 cent arbitrage profit whatever the eventual spot rate on expiry.

The same construction could be put together using different option strike combinations, for example:

Buy sterling forward at $1.59
Sell $1.55 call for 7 cents
Buy $1.55 put for 2 cents

Alternatively:

Buy sterling forward at $1.59
Sell $1.65 call for 2 cents
Buy $1.65 put for 7 cents

Both combinations produce the effect of selling sterling forward at $1.60, which results in an arbitrage opportunity against the real forward outright.

The opposite trade, selling the currency forward, selling a put and buying a call, is known as a 'forward reversal'. This is a combination of a forward sale and a synthetic long. Thus:

Sell sterling at $1.61
Buy $1.60 call for 4 cents
Sell $1.60 put for 4 cents

Such a trade will result in a profit of 1 cent wherever sterling trades on the expiry date of the option.

In reality, in an efficient market forward conversions and reversals should be marginally impossible; any arbitrage opportunity should be squeezed out in the bid/ask spread. Nevertheless this pricing relationship between calls and puts remains consistent and can be defined as follows: a European currency put option has the same premium as a European currency call option with the same strike and maturity less the difference between the forward rate and the strike.

This pricing relationship, put-call parity, can be expressed thus:

Call premium $-$ put premium $=$ Forward $-$ strike.

For example, with sterling forward at $1.60:

If the $1.55 call premium	=	7 cents,
The $1.55 put premium	=	7 cents − ($1.60−$1.55)
	=	7 cents − 5 cents
	=	2 cents

Similarly, with sterling forward at $1.60:

If the $1.65 call premium	=	2 cents,
The $1.65 put premium	=	2 cents − ($1.60−$1.65)
	=	2 cents + 5 cents
	=	7 cents

Synthetics

If a synthetic long can be constructed by buying a call and writing a put option, or a synthetic short results from buying a put and writing a call, other combinations of options and forwards can be put together to make up different forms of synthetics. Some, although by no means a comprehensive list, are given below:

1. Long forward + Long put = Synthetic long call
    e.g. Buy sterling forward at $1.60
        Buy $1.55 put for 2 cents.
    The exposure is exactly the same as buying a $1.55 call for 7 cents.

    For example, assume spot rate on expiry is $1.75.

    Synthetic call position:
Forward profit = $1.75 − $1.60	=	15 cents
Put option abandoned. Cost	=	2 cents
Net profit from synthetic	=	13 cents

    $1.55 call option position:
$1.55 call worth $1.75 − $1.55	=	20 cents
Less cost of call option	=	7 cents
Net profit from call option	=	13 cents.

2. Short forward + Short put = Synthetic short call
    e.g. Sell sterling forward at $1.60
        Sell $1.60 put for 4 cents.
    The exposure is exactly the same as selling a $1.60 call for 4 cents.

3. Short forward + Long call = Synthetic long put
    e.g. Sell sterling forward at $1.60
        Buy $1.60 call for 4 cents.
    The exposure is exactly the same as buying a $1.60 put for 4 cents.

4. Long forward + Short call = Synthetic short put
    e.g. Buy sterling forward at $1.60
        Sell $1.60 call for 4 cents.
    The exposure is exactly the same as selling a $1.60 put for 4 cents.

It is always possible to convert a long put into a long call option, or, vice versa, through a forward trade; e.g.

Convert long $1.55 call into long $1.55 put:
sell sterling forward at $1.60

Convert short $1.65 call into short $1.65 put:
buy sterling forward at $1.60

Convert long $1.60 put into long $1.60 call:
buy sterling forward at $1.60

Convert short $1.65 put into short $1.65 call:
sell sterling forward at $1.60.

It is possible to convert long puts into long calls, for example, or short calls into short puts; however, it is not possible to convert a short option into a long option position; nor is it possible to convert a long option into a short option position.

Synthetics are important, not because of possible arbitrage opportunities, which are rare, but because an understanding of synthetics leads to a more thorough knowledge of the market. Moreover, in circumstances where calls and puts are priced differently it may be possible to create a synthetic option more cheaply than an outright.

For example, when a currency is well-offered or bid, speculative action may well distort the premium levels. For example, with forward sterling at $1.60, in circumstances where the pound is under selling pressure the following price relationships may hold:

Sterling forward: $1.60
$1.59 put option quote: 4.25–4.50 (cents)
$1.59 call option quote: 5.00–5.25 (cents)

No arbitrage opportunity is available here; a forward reversal would be possible if one could buy the $1.59 call at 5.25 cents, sell the $1.59 put at 4.50 cents, and sell sterling forward at $1.60, resulting in a locked-in arbitrage profit of 0.25 cents.[4]

Sentiment in the market has pushed up the price of sterling puts in relation to sterling calls, but the arbitrage opportunity is lost in the bid/ ask spread. Nevertheless, for an option trader intending to buy sterling put options, a better strategy would be to buy the $1.59 call for 5.25 cents, and sell sterling forward at $1.60. Remember:

---

[4] Remember: call premium − put premium = forward − strike
Therefore, $1.59 put premium = call premium − (forward − strike)
$$= 5.25 - (\$1.60 - \$1.59)$$
$$= 5.25 - 1.00$$
$$= 4.25$$
The $1.59 put premium, therefore, should be 4.25 cents, not 4.50 cents.

Short forward + long call = synthetic long put
Synthetic put premium = call premium − (forward − strike)
= $0.0525 − ($1.60 − $1.59)
= 4.25 cents

This converts the long call into a long put option costing 4.25 cents, which is 0.25 cents cheaper than the simple put option purchase. Such opportunities occur regularly in the market-place.

PART TWO

Hedging foreign exchange risk using currency options

In many ways the idea of separating currency traders and hedgers into two distinct groups with little or nothing in common is an over-simplification. The inference is that on the one hand there exists a number of speculators who regularly 'bet the house' on the next move in the dollar, while on the other hand there are those who use the foreign exchange markets purely to hedge a currency exposure. In reality the distinction is blurred. The speculator who, in anticipation of a weak economic number, reduces his long dollar/Deutschmark position by selling some dollar/yen (and converts his position into a partial cross-rate) is hedging his risk. Similarly, take the case of the Japanese exporter of video cassette recorders to the United States who will receive dollars on the future delivery date and is therefore exposed to a fall in the dollar versus the yen between now and the day the shipment is received; he cannot avoid taking what is effectively a trading or speculative view on the movement in the currency. Either he hedges by selling his dollars forward, and risks losing a windfall profit should the dollar rally, or he does nothing in anticipation of being able to sell his dollars higher on the delivery date, and risks making a loss should the dollar fall. In other words, the very decision whether or not to hedge is a trading decision, and is unavoidable.

There are many participants in the foreign exchange markets: commercial and investment banks, corporations, international fund managers, central banks and private individuals; some of these act as market-makers, as traders, as arbitrageurs, or as hedgers. But the differences between these groups is mainly a matter of semantics. For the purposes of this section the traditional distinction of trader and hedger has been retained for the sake of convenience; a trader being defined as one who uses the market for speculative gain and a hedger, one who uses the market to avoid a speculative risk. But in practice there is often little to choose between the two.

CHAPTER 5

Why hedge with currency options?

Foreign exchange risk

Exposure to movements in foreign exchange rates and currency market volatility can be an advantage (few foreign exchange traders would derive any income without it), but for many corporate treasurers and international fund managers it is regarded as anything from a niggling nuisance to a major financial headache. Take the example of a Japanese audio-visual manufacturer who exports to the United States and who will receive US dollars as payment against delivery in three months' time. If the US dollar falls against the yen by the payment date the profit margin on the deal will be eroded; if the dollar fall is large enough the manufacturer will make a loss. Alternatively, if the dollar were to rally substantially within three months the exporter will have made large windfall profits on his dollar receivables.

 Since the demise of the Bretton Woods agreement in the 1970s the classic method of hedging such transaction risks has been to sell US dollars in the forward foreign exchange market. (In the 1960s such techniques as parallel and back-to-back loans achieved the same end result.) However, the process of selling dollars forward hedges away any potential profits as well as losses. Windfall gains, such as would have resulted from a rise in the $/yen rate, are also eliminated.[1]

Usually the decision whether to trade the forward market, hedging the

---

[1] In practice, two other solutions might be useful to the Japanese manufacturer. Firstly, the invoice and the payment could be made in Japanese yen rather than in US dollars. Of course, even assuming this would be acceptable to the American importer, the currency risk will not have been eliminated, only transferred from the Japanese to the American company, who would now have committed themselves to pay Japanese yen in three months' time; the American importer could hedge his yen payables by buying yen in the forward foreign exchange market. Secondly, if the dollar depreciation is sufficiently severe, or of long enough duration, the Japanese manufacturer might decide to relocate some production to the United States. (However, while this might eliminate transaction risk from the manufacturer's point of view, it would inevitably create a translation exposure for the Japanese parent company, regarding the profits or losses of its US subsidiary.)

risk but eliminating any potential gains, or to do nothing, risking large transaction losses for the opportunity of making large windfall profits, is a matter of risk tolerance. According to the conventional definition the hedger differs from the speculator in that he is risk averse; a trader accepts risk, welcomes it indeed, whereas the priority of the hedger is to reduce or eliminate currency exposure. But in reality the attitude to foreign exchange risk among corporate treasurers and fund managers is wide-ranging. Some corporations are fairly relaxed about foreign exchange management, content to place considerable responsibility on the shoulders of the corporate treasurer's department; some multinationals act as banks to their subsidiaries, and 'trade' their hedges actively in the inter-bank market. At the other end of the spectrum, some corporations regard any foreign exchange risk with alarm, and mechanically hedge any currency exposure in the forward market as soon as it occurs. There are also a surprising number of corporations who never use the forward foreign exchange market and who treat subsequent windfall profits or losses as virtually an 'act of God'.

Similarly, among fund managers an argument is continually being fought between those who regard the currency risk associated with investing overseas as an integral part of the investment decision itself and those who differentiate between the economic performance of a country in the long term and the stock market/bond market/currency risk in the short term. For example, take this extract from a letter to the *Financial Times* of 29 April 1985 from C. E. Hughes, Managing Director of Provident Mutual Managed Pension Funds:

'Turning to the question of currency hedging, there may well be a long-term positive correlation between economic performance, currency values and indeed stock market prices, but the variations about any such long-term trend are large in size and extended in time. Furthermore, the variations in currency value from the trend are not necessarily coincident in direction and time with the variations in stock market prices. The investment manager's job is surely to act on his judgment about overvaluation or undervaluation of the assets in which he invests. I see no reason why he should not take a different view as between the currency and the underlying equity, stock or bond and act accordingly. For instance, I see no distinction in principle between a decision to sell US stocks and hold the cash realised in US dollars and a decision to hedge part of a US dollar portfolio.'

More recently, on 28 March 1987, the *Independent* carried an article headed 'US fund's dollar dilemma', which described how the 25 best performing US invested unit trusts had shown returns of between 13 per cent and 15 per cent (offer to offer) for the year to date; by comparison the Dow Jones Industrial Average had risen nearly 30 per cent during the same period. The rally in sterling of about 10 per cent against the US dollar was made the scapegoat for this poor investment performance. The

Independent asked some fund managers whether they should have hedged; one was quoted as saying

'We weren't and aren't hedged. It is our policy that we shouldn't be. We believe that when a client invests in US securities he should be aware he should be taking a dollar risk as well.'

Other fund managers took a similar view, although they had hedged in the past. Other managers believed in hedging but were restricted by the terms of the trust deed.

As a measure of how currency performance can affect an international fund, see Table 5.1 for world bond market performance in 1985 and 1986.

From a US dollar investor's point of view, the strong performance of sterling bonds in 1985 and the dismal record the following year can be put down almost entirely to currency factors. In 1985, the two best performing markets in local currency terms, US dollars and Canadian dollars, finished virtually bottom of the international league table, above only the

Table 5.1. International Eurobond market-performance.

Performance in 1985[1] Total rate of return		
Bond market	Performance in US $ terms (%)	Performance in local currency terms (%)
Guilder	44	11
Deutschmark	43	11
Ecu	42	14
Sterling	40	13
Yen	39	11
Swiss franc	35	7
US $	19	19
Canadian $	14	21
Australian $	−7	13

Performance in 1986 Total rate of return		
Bond market	Performance in US $ terms (%)	Performance in local currency terms (%)
Yen	36	10
Deutschmark	34	6
Ecu	32	10
Guilder	31	6
US $	14	14
Australian $	13	16
Canadian $	12	10
Sterling	11	10

Note:
1. Source AIBD; Merrill Lynch (all percentages to nearest whole figure).

very weak Australian dollar which finished a poor ninth. In 1985 and 1986 the impressive performance of all the major currency bond markets was due once again to the currency factor; in local currency terms the US dollar gave the second highest returns in both years (three times that of the Swiss franc bond market in 1985 for example), but finished a poor seventh in the international table in 1985 and a poor fifth in 1986. Currency, indeed, was the key as far as the international bond investor was concerned.

It is this very unpredictable nature of foreign exchange movements and the resulting problems for the corporate treasurer or fund manager which has, in recent years, led to the development of a liquid currency options market, not, as some have suggested, as another interesting off-balance sheet trading vehicle, but to satisfy the demands of end users anxious to find a more suitable means of covering foreign exchange risk.

Options versus spot versus forwards

To illustrate the currency hedging alternatives available, let us return to the case of the Japanese manufacturer who, on exporting $50 million worth of cameras and other equipment to the United States, was risking a falling dollar which might erode or eliminate his profit margin on the sale.

With the spot $/yen at yen 155 and the three months forward rate at yen 154, the treasurer could hedge his currency by selling $50 million at the forward outright rate. However, by hedging his 'long' dollar position he has, at the same time, eliminated any potential currency gains. Assuming that after three months the US dollar is either 10 yen higher, 10 yen lower, or unchanged, the manufacturer's exposure profile would look as follows:

Day one: spot $/yen 155. Forward $/yen 154.
Action one: do nothing. Wait until the dollars are received in three months' time and then sell them at the prevailing spot rate.

Action two: hedge. Sell $50 million in the forward market at yen 154.

Foreign exchange rate achieved in three months' time:

	Spot $/yen		
	145	155	165
Hedged:	154	154	154
Unhedged:	145	155	165

To summarise, the forward hedge fixes the rate; this could be attractive to the corporate treasurer because he will know in advance exactly the yen value of his dollar receivables. He may perhaps be totally indifferent to the subsequent movement of the dollar, up or down, but most likely he will regret having hedged should the dollar rally substantially (as in the example), particularly if his major competitors have not hedged and therefore will be able to profit – at his expense – from a rising dollar. But while hedging has the disadvantage of inflexibility, the decision not to hedge – running the currency exposure – is an open ended risk leading to potentially large gains or large losses.

As an alternative, the corporate treasurer considers the option strategy. He buys a three months yen 155 call option (US dollar put) for about 2 per cent or 3 yen. The results after a similar spot move over three months would look as follows:

Action three: buy yen call option. Buy three months yen 155 (at-the-money) call for 3 yen.

Foreign exchange rate achieved in three months' time:

	Spot $/yen		
	145	155	165
Option	152	152	162
strategy			

The cost of the call option is equivalent to 3 yen; this is the amount by which the currency has to move in order to recapture the cost of the premium paid. The dollar has to rise to above 158 yen or fall to below 152 yen by expiry for the strategy to be effective. Should the dollar fall to Y145 by the time the dollars are received, the treasurer will either exercise the option, allowing him to sell dollars at the original strike price of Y155, or sell it back for its intrinsic value and sell the dollars spot. In either case he will have achieved a net rate of Y152 (Y155 − Y3). Should the yen be unchanged the treasurer may, if he wishes, still exercise the call option, but because the option has already been bought his net rate remains at Y152. In such a case the option purchase would have been the incorrect strategy because the premium has effectively been paid away for nothing. However, in insurance terms the corporate treasurer may well be happy to have risked 3 yen in order to protect himself on any dollar sell-off.

Because the treasurer has bought a yen call option which gives him the right, not the obligation, to buy the currency at the strike price, he will only exercise that right should the yen be higher than the strike by expiration day. If the yen falls in value (the dollar rallies) to Y165 in three months' time the treasurer will certainly not exercise his option; he will let the option expire worthless and instead sell his dollars/buy yen at the more attractive spot rate. The net rate he achieves will be the rate he sells dollars less the original premium he has already paid away. In our example the net rate is Y162; he sells his dollar receivables in the spot market at Y165 but has already paid 3 yen away for the option.

Were the corporate treasurer relatively relaxed about his long dollar position he might be happy to run his exposure in the spot market. However, either to assuage a nervous board of directors, or to put a stop-loss on his position in the event of an unforeseen disaster, he could look at the idea of buying the equivalent of disaster insurance – an out-of-the-money option. In this case he buys a Y150 three month call option for 1 yen.

> Action four: buy out-of-the-money yen call option. Buy three months Y150 call for 1 yen.

> Foreign exchange rate achieved in three months' time:

> Spot $/yen
> | | | |
> |---|---|---|
> | 145 | 155 | 165 |
> | 149 | 154 | 164 |

The out-of-the-money option is cheaper, but gives less protection; the at-the-money option is more expensive but gives better protection. On any large rally in the yen the at-the-money call would have proved the better investment. On any fall, the out-of-the-money option would have been preferable. Of course, the choice of strikes is open to the buyer; on the exchanges he has a fixed range from which to choose; in the OTC market the choice is virtually limitless; but the decision itself is based on the treasurer's view of the market and tolerance to risk.

A decision tree could be constructed to reflect the treasurer's view of the market and his tolerance to risk (see Table 5.2).

Table 5.2. Currency hedging decision tree. (Corporate treasurer has currency payables.)

View of currency	View of risk	Action
Very bullish	risk averse	buy currency forward
Very bullish	risk tolerant	buy currency forward
Bullish	risk averse	buy currency forward
Bullish	risk tolerant	buy atm[1] call
Flat market	risk averse	do nothing or buy ootm call[2]
Flat market	risk tolerant	do nothing
No view	risk averse	buy atm call
No view	risk tolerant	do nothing or buy atm call
Bearish	risk averse	buy ootm call
Bearish	risk tolerant	do nothing
Very bearish	risk averse	do nothing or buy far ootm call
Very bearish	risk tolerant	do nothing

Notes:
1. atm = at-the-money.
2. ootm = out-of-the-money.

Are options expensive?

It has to be said at the outset that for the hedger, the option alternative can never be the best strategy. With the benefit of hindsight the optimum strategy is either to trade the currency forward or to leave the exposure unhedged until the transaction becomes spot. However, while the option is never the best strategy, it is usually only marginally less effective than the best, and a substantial improvement on the worst strategy.

Take, for example, a UK exporter to the United States who has dollar receivables and is therefore at risk if the dollar falls/sterling rallies. This might be a corporation such as Jaguar or Glaxo, or indeed a UK fund manager investing in US equities or bonds. Unhedged, the exposure will result in large transaction profits if sterling falls, and equally large losses if sterling rallies. Given the violent fluctuations in the sterling/dollar rate in recent years the corporate treasurer/fund manager has been faced with some very difficult decisions.

In March 1984 sterling was trading at $1.50 but within 12 months had fallen by 30 per cent to a low of $1.05. In a perfect world, the best strategy for the treasurer in early 1984 would have been to have avoided the forward market entirely and to have sold his dollar receivables (bought his pounds) in the spot market; even better would have been to have held these receipts in US dollar form and thus to have continued to have profited from a falling pound.

By March/April of 1986 sterling had bounced back strongly from the lows and was trading above $1.50 once again. In this case the optimum strategy would have been to have hedged for the whole year, to have bought sterling one year forward in the spring of 1985 in order to cover all the dollar receivables for the next 12 months. (Ideally he should have over-hedged, if at all possible.) In fact, the one year forward outright price for sterling in March 1985 was close to $1.00; thus the treasurer could have bought his pounds at near parity with the dollar and then sat back and watched as sterling rallied over 50 per cent in the next 12 months.

It should be remembered that, in the early part of 1985, many forecasters were predicting a continuing collapse of sterling – levels of $0.85 or $0.90 were mentioned at the time; the optimum strategy for the treasurer to have adopted, therefore, would have been to have taken the opposite view of popular market opinion. Of course, popular opinion is often very wrong; for example, the oil price collapse in early 1986 was expected to bring about a major sell-off in sterling; instead, after flirting with the $1.40 level in the autumn of 1986, by March 1987 sterling had recovered strongly and was forging into new high ground around the $1.60 level. At this stage the Bank of England was selling sterling to prevent the currency from moving any higher. The optimum strategy for the treasurer in the spring of 1986, therefore, would have again been to have bought sterling in the forward market (ideally, he should have left the position unhedged until sterling fell to $1.40 and then should have bought forward).

Table 5.3 is an illustration of how a treasurer should ideally have managed his exposure for the 12 months following the beginning of his financial year (March) for the years 1984, 1985, and 1986. By comparison the worst strategy as well as the option alternative is also included. The illustration assumes that the treasurer anticipates receiving $100 million each year and that the cost of a one year sterling call/dollar put is 5 per cent ($5 million) in each case.

On balance, the option strategy was never the best, but for two out of three years, it was a substantial improvement over the worst strategy. Only for 1986 was the logic of buying sterling call options questionable in that the premium paid, again with the benefit of hindsight, was high given the relatively small movement in sterling after 12 months' duration. Even here, however, the strategy of buying options would have been an improvement over the worst strategy of leaving the position unhedged.

In conclusion it may be said that for a corporate treasurer or fund manager with a proven record of successful foreign exchange market forecasting, who is confident that his view of the direction of the market is the right one, there is little place for options in his armoury of foreign exchange trading tools; he should simply back his judgement and trade accordingly. In the real world, however, surely no one can afford to be so

Table 5.3. Exposure management.

---

1. March 1984   March 1985
   Spot $1.50   Spot $1.05
   Optimum strategy: buy $100 MM spot. Gain: $30 million
   Worst strategy: buy $100 MM forward. Loss $30 million
   Option strategy: buy $100 MM one year $1.50 call for $5MM
   Option strategy results: net gain = $25 million

2. March 1985   March 1986
   Spot $1.05   Spot $1.50
   Optimum strategy: buy $100 MM forward. Gain: $43 million
   Worst strategy: buy $100 MM spot. Loss: $43 million
   Option strategy: buy $100 MM one year $1.05 call for $5 MM
   Option strategy results: net gain = $38 million

3. March 1986   March 1987
   Spot $1.50   Spot $1.60
   Optimum strategy: buy $100 MM forward. Gain: $6.6 million
   Worst strategy: buy $100 MM spot. Loss: $6.6 million
   Option strategy: buy $100 MM one year $1.50 call for $5 MM
   Option strategy results: net gain = $1.6 MM

---

confident. Nowadays, political events as well as economic data affect exchange rates, and there are as many interpretations of the data itself as there are economists. Buying options is like buying car insurance – car insurance is always expensive except, of course, in the unforeseen event of an accident.

Disadvantages of currency options

In 1984 an official at the Bank of England was reported as saying that eventually some 50 per cent of currency forward hedging requirements for corporations and fund managers would be met by currency options. Yet although the market has indeed grown substantially in recent years not even the most optimistic proponent could claim a corporate involvement of anything approaching this level. Having pointed out some of the many advantages in using the currency option market it needs to be asked at this stage what factors have proved an impediment to further growth in the product. They conclude the following:

1. Many corporations who mark all their foreign exchange transactions to the market, have great problems in valuing their options positions, particularly those in the over-the-counter market. It is not simply possible, as it would be with a spot foreign exchange position, to take OTC options prices from a Reuters or Telerate screen or from the *Wall Street Journal*; either the corporate treasurer has to value the position himself using his own computer software or he has to rely on a daily valuation from a bank or currency option broker. Very often he either does not have suitable software or there is a lack of personnel with sufficient time to manipulate it properly. (The software itself is easily available but the inputs for the pricing model – particularly implied volatility – still have to be obtained from the market.) Of course, accurate and up-to-date options prices can be found in the news services for exchange traded currency options; but the disadvantage here, apart from any inherent inflexibility in the listed market itself, is that many corporations have serious difficulties coping with and monitoring the initial and variation margin payments on short option positions.

2. The very wide-ranging number of hedging opportunities and strategies open to the treasurer in the currency options market can itself be a disadvantage; not only is the decision-making process made more complex by the addition of various option strategies, but many treasurers are deeply sceptical of some of these more exotic strategies that are being marketed.

3. Treasurers are concerned about the level of liquidity in the market, and confused by reports of widely varying prices from different

banks. In theory, of course, corporations can arbitrage between banks' prices if they are out of line – and some do; but more often the inconvenience of tying up available credit lines outweighs any short-term profit advantages.
4.   Rumours of heavy losses suffered by currency option market-makers from time to time has undermined confidence in the market.

Some of these objections may explain why options were not used in one of the most celebrated case studies in recent years, that of Lufthansa.

The Lufthansa case

In the early months of 1985 Lufthansa purchased 20 Boeing 737 aeroplanes from the American manufacturers at a total cost of about $500 million. The spot $/DM rate,which at that time was about DM 3.20, was soon to peak at around DM 3.45 following an extended rally which had confounded many currency market forecasters. The $500 million was due to be paid on the delivery date of the aeroplanes in a year's time; this left the board of Lufthansa with the problem of what to do about their forthcoming US dollar payables.

Three strategies were examined; firstly, running the dollar 'short' position in the hope of a dollar fall over the next twelve months; secondly, covering in the forward market at the prevailing rate; and thirdly, buying a Deutschmark put (US dollar call) option as insurance and running the spot position. Because of the high premium cost (about 6 per cent) and therefore the large outlay for the option premium (about $30 million), and also because of some doubts about the liquidity of the market at that time, Lufthansa decided not to pursue the option strategy. The conservative alternative would have been to have bought dollars forward (the exposure would have been hedged, after all, and the Deutschmark cost would have been known in advance), but Lufthansa felt that a dollar decline was imminent and therefore decided instead to cover 50 per cent of the exposure in the forward market, and to run the remaining 50 per cent of the 'short' position.

As events developed, Lufthansa's decision not to hedge all their forward requirements proved correct as the US dollar plunged from a high of over DM 3.40 down to DM 2.30 within twelve months. The reaction inside West Germany, however, was far from temperate. When it was revealed that the decision to cover 50 per cent of the position in the forward market had cost Lufthansa over DM 200 million, or to put it another way, had Lufthansa not hedged any forward dollars they would have made further windfall profits in excess of DM 200 million, there was a political storm. According to the *Financial Times* of 24 February 1986, Herr Heinz Ruhnau 'was summoned to meet Mr Werner Dollinger, the

Transport Minister, to explain the losses. Unconfirmed reports were circulating here this weekend that a decision by the airline's supervisory board on whether to extend his term of office when it expires in 1987 would be postponed until at least June.' In fact there were newspaper stories that political rivals had demanded Herr Ruhnau's dismissal 'for reckless speculation'. Yet most neutrals would have viewed the decision not to hedge 50 per cent of the exposure, in other words, to have run a 'short' dollar position of $250 million for twelve months, as 'speculative' and potentially very dangerous.

The Lufthansa case is illuminating in that it shows how the decision to choose what may appear to be the conservative and prudent strategy rather than the speculative one can often blow up in the face of the corporate treasurer. Whether or not 6 per cent was too large a premium to pay for a 12-month option (obviously not, given the subsequent fall in the dollar) or whether Lufthansa might have considered buying out-of-the-money options, or one of the numerous combinations available involving the buying and writing of options in order to reduce or eliminate the premium cost, is not the main issue. Indeed, it may well be that the liquidity in the option market in early 1985 was not sufficient to handle the sort of size that Lufthansa would have needed to have traded. What is certain, however, is that the market today is well capable of absorbing such a volume of business, and given the variety of 'fine-tuning' strategies at hand either in the option market itself or as offered by banks in a 'packaged' form, there is no longer any reason for corporate treasurers to ignore the opportunities that are made available to them through the currency options market.

When the Philadelphia Stock Exchange began marketing their new product, exchange traded currency options, in 1982, they hit upon the apt slogan: 'currency options, the third dimension to foreign exchange'. The currency options market has indeed opened up the horizons of the corporate treasurer and international fund manager. To quote Mr William T. Lawrence, foreign exchange manager in the banking division at Hercules Incorporated, an international speciality chemicals and aerospace manufacturer:[2]

'I think the usage of options is going to continue to grow because of the volatility of the market and the fundamental problem that you have in hedging. It's easy enough to hedge the risk. It is an insurance function, and the analogy to the house is a good one: you insure your house for $100,000 against the possibility of it burning down. But if it doesn't burn down, you want to be able to sell it for

---

[2] Interview in sponsored supplement to *Intermarket*, November 1986, by the Philadelphia Stock Exchange.

$110,000 or $120,000, if that's what the market is worth at the time you are ready to sell.

But under the standard form of hedging in foreign currencies – forward contracts – you hedge at, let's say a pound at $1.25, and it goes to $1.50. You're stuck still with $1.25. You can't sell it at the higher value. On the other hand, if you have the option, like insurance, you're still free to reap the windfall gain.'

Advantages of currency options

From a hedging point of view currency options can have other advantages. For one, the date on which the currency is to be paid or received, or the precise amount of currency required, may not be known. A forward hedge is often too exact in these circumstances, but the peculiar structure of an option, that it confers rights on the buyer but no obligations, allows the purchaser to set his own terms on the transaction. He can buy an option for a date slightly longer than the likely delivery period and for an amount which he knows will cover his requirements. The cost of a longer-dated option and for a larger amount than may be necessary will obviously be higher, but only marginally so; the longer the maturity, the less impact this will have.

Moreover, when options are purchased in a tender-to-contract situation where the corporation has a contingent rather than a fixed need to buy or sell currency, a windfall profit may result should the tender not be accepted but the currency move in the option's favour. For example, if the tender is for a bid on a foreign contract the corporation might buy a put on the currency to hedge the contingent receipts; should the tender not be accepted the option may be sold for any residual value it may have. If it is out-of-the-money and near expiration the option will be virtually worthless; but if the currency falls during the tender period the put will be in-the-money and can be sold for at least its intrinsic value, resulting in windfall profits for the hedger. Such returns may offset the premium losses on other tender situations when the bid is not accepted and the option expires worthless.

Another advantage of the option product is for small companies who have no access to the forward market because they are insufficiently capitalised to be allowed a forward foreign exchange line; alternatively they may trade in such small quantities, or so infrequently, that the spreads on which they have to deal are very wide. The attraction of the options market – and here the advantage is very much with the exchanges rather than the OTC market – is that the contract size is small, and the same price usually exists for one contract as for fifty. Buying listed currency options is sometimes the only effective way for smaller companies to be able to access the foreign exchange market, particularly the forward market. While buying or selling currency forward requires a foreign exchange line, anyone can buy a currency option regardless of his credit rating.

But probably the main attraction of currency options is that the corporate treasurer or fund manager can put together a variety of strategies which will adequately reflect his view of the market and his tolerance of risk. The keystone of these strategies is the ability to write as well as to buy currency options.

CHAPTER 6

Option hedging techniques involving buying and writing

Why write options?

The logic behind the concept of buying and writing options in order to hedge a foreign exchange exposure derived originally from corporate treasurers who complained about the apparent high cost of the option premium; the obvious retort to such complaints was 'If you think options are too expensive then write them!' But by putting together combinations of options, bought and sold, the treasurer discovered that not only had he constructed a product which fell somewhere between an option and a forward, but by varying the strikes he could adjust his position to match his required exposure.

For example, with sterling at $1.50, a corporate treasurer or fund manager with US dollar receivables to hedge might buy a $1.50 sterling call for 5.5 cents, or buy a $1.55 call for 3.5 cents. Either strategy might appear attractive, except for the fact that the premium has still to be paid, and most treasurers or investment managers are loth to part with what may turn out to be unnecessary funds. Therefore, as an alternative to simply buying the $1.55 call, the hedger simultaneously writes a $1.40 put. In this case, the premium he receives from writing the put exactly matches the premium he pays for the $1.55 call. The treasurer has created what is known sometimes as a zero cost fence, a cylinder option, a forward spread, a range contract or a fox-collar (the names of these products vary according to the bank offering them but the structure is very much the same). However, by writing the put to pay for the call option, the hedger no longer has the simple exposure to the market achieved by an outright purchase. The call he has purchased gives him the right to buy sterling at $1.55; but the put he has written gives him the obligation to buy sterling at $1.40. The results can be expressed as in Table 6.1.

Table 6.1. Hedging strategies: long call and 'fence'.

Spot sterling $1.50
$1.55 12 month call (European) 3.5 cents. $1.40 put 3.5 cents

Strategy 1: Long call
Buy $1.55 call for 3.5 cents

Strategy 2: 'Fence'
Buy $1.55 call for 3.5 cents/write $1.45 put for 3.5 cents

Results on expiry: Spot rate:	Long call	Fence
$1.25	Abandon call option and buy sterling spot: net rate = $1.25 + $0.035 = $1.2850	Assigned $1.40 put: buy sterling at $1.40
$1.50	Abandon call option and buy sterling spot: net rate = $1.50 + $0.035 = $1.5350	Abandon call (put option also expires) buy spot at $1.50 net rate = $1.50
$1.75	Exercise $1.55 call: receive sterling at $1.55 net rate = $1.55 + $0.035 = $1.5850	Exercise $1.55 call: receive sterling at $1.55 (strike price) net rate = $1.55

Thus on expiry, if sterling is above $1.55 the call option in both cases will be exercised; if between $1.55 and $1.40 in both cases the call option is abandoned and sterling can be bought at the prevailing spot rate. Below $1.40 the call option buyer also abandons his option and sells dollars/ buys sterling spot; the 'fence' trade commits the put writer to buy sterling at $1.40, however; below this rate the put will be assigned, thus forcing the put writer to honour his obligation to buy sterling at the strike price.

The 'fence' is a half-way house between an option and a forward. Its advantage is that the upside is protected in the same way as any normal call option, but because there is no premium to pay the break-even rate is exactly the same as the strike, in this case $1.55. The trade-off is that in order to pay for the call the hedger has written a put option which commits him to buy sterling at $1.40 should the pound fall to this level.[1] This would not be very attractive were sterling to fall to, say, $1.20, but the hedger would at least have the consolation that he bought pounds lower than the rate at which he could originally have traded the forward outright, and that he parted with no premium money.

It has to be stated, of course, that such a strategy should only be constructed if the currency really indeed needs to be purchased; it would not be appropriate with a contingent risk such as in a tender situation,

[1] In all these examples European options are written so that there is no risk of early assignment.

because should the tender fail the hedger would be left with a similar exposure as if he had bought sterling forward; if sterling collapsed and the tender failed he would be left with an unwanted sterling long position.

But for normal hedging requirements the fence strategy has much to be said for it. Firstly, the hedger can adjust the strikes around the spot to reflect different exposure requirements; he could, for example, construct a similar fence with strikes at $1.51 for the call and $1.44 for the put, or at $1.60 for the call and $1.36 for the put; the former would give him a reasonably tight range with good upside protection but only a limited amount of profit potential on the downside; the latter gives the hedger the chance to make substantial profits on any major sell-off in sterling but risks greater losses on any rally.

Nor does the fence have to be constructed at zero cost; it can be put together for a small debit. Buying a $1.52 call and writing a $1.41 put, for example, would have a net cost of only 0.5 cents premium, but would allow the hedger the opportunity of greater profits on any fall in sterling. Alternatively, buying a $1.52 call and writing a $1.43 put would give the hedger a small credit of 0.5 cents; this gives him the same protection on the upside, but will also provide him with additional income should sterling stabilise.

Hedging strategies

The variations that can be put together involving the buying and/or writing of currency options gives the corporate treasurer or fund manager an enormously wide range of possibilities with which to 'fine tune' his currency exposure. Here are a few examples of possible strategies:

Scenario: A corporate treasurer anticipates receiving US dollars in one year's time. He is sterling based and is therefore at risk if the dollar falls/sterling rises by the time the dollars are received.

Spot sterling: $1.50

One year forward outright: $1.46

Strategy 1: Do nothing. (Wait until the dollars are received and then sell them spot.)

Comments: While making good profits on any sterling decline, the position is likely to incur substantial losses on any rally.

Strategy 2: Buy sterling forward at $1.46.

Comments: While this has the advantage of locking in a forward rate at a discount to the spot and will fully protect the position should sterling rally, there is no opportunity to benefit from any decline in sterling.

Strategy 3: Buy $1.50 call option for 5.5 cents.

Comments: This is akin to buying insurance. For the strategy to be effective sterling must either rise above $1.5550 or fall below $1.4450 to cover the cost of the option premium. The strategy works well in any widely swinging market, therefore. Should sterling collapse the option can be abandoned and the hedger will be able to take advantage of any windfall profit opportunities (less the cost of the premium, of course). At the same time the option provides protection above the break-even rate of $1.5550.

Strategy 4: Buy $1.55 call option for 3.5 cents.

Comments: In insurance terms, buying an out-of-the-money call option is like buying fire or disaster insurance. The cost is small but so is the protection; on a net basis he is covered above $1.5850 only. It would be best employed if the treasurer felt confident that sterling was going down but wanted to retain some protection in case of unforeseen events.

Strategy 5: Write $1.50 put option for 9 cents.

Comments: Writing a put option instead of buying a call has the advantage in a standstill market where the premium received can be offset against the purchase cost of sterling. For example, if sterling in one year's time is at $1.45, the put option will be assigned, which means that the treasurer will have been given sterling at $1.50; however, his net purchase rate will be the strike less the original premium received, $1.50 less 9 cents, or $1.41. If sterling should fall precipitously, however, say to $1.25, he will still have bought the currency on a net basis at $1.41. On the other hand, while the premium received will act as a cushion on any rally in sterling, the level of protection is small. At $1.55, for example, the treasurer's net purchase rate for sterling is $1.55 less 9 cents, or $1.46; at $1.75 he will have bought sterling net at $1.75 less 9 cents, or $1.66. A useful strategy in a sideways market, therefore, but offering little real protection or opportunity to make windfall profits.

Strategy 6: Buy a $1.50 call for 5.5 cents.
Write a $1.57 call for 2.5 cents.

Comments: The attraction of this strategy is that by buying a spread rather than an outright option the treasurer has reduced his up-front cost from 5.5 cents to 3 cents. The trade-off, of course, is that protection ends at $1.57, because of the short $1.57 call. The net profit on the spread at $1.57 or above is 4 cents (the difference between the strikes less the initial premium cost). Thus if sterling rallies strongly, say to $1.75, the treasurer's net purchase rate is reduced by only 4 cents, to $1.71. Again, this is a strategy for relatively stable markets, not one to be recommended in volatile conditions.

Strategy 7: Buy a $1.55 call option for 3.5 cents.
Write a $1.40 put option for 3.5 cents.

Comments: This strategy, a zero cost fence, has the advantage of giving upside protection close to the spot rate and allows good profit potential on any large sterling sell-off. Its main disadvantage is that very large windfall profits are not possible because of the limiting factor of the short $1.40 put position.

Strategy 8: Buy a $1.60 call option for 2.5 cents.
Write a $1.36 put option for 2.5 cents.

Comments: Another zero cost fence, but with much wider parameters. The treasurer sacrifices good upside protection for the opportunity of making substantial windfall profits on any decline in sterling (down to $1.36).

Strategy 9: Buy a $1.51 call option for 5 cents.
Write a $1.44 put option for 5 cents.

Comments: A zero cost fence but with tighter parameters. Upside protection is very good but in this case the trade-off for the treasurer is limited profit potential on any fall in the pound.

Strategy 10: Buy a $1.52 call option for 4.5 cents.
Write a $1.41 put option for 4 cents.

Comments: In this case the fence is constructed for a small debit of 0.5 cents. The effect of paying some premium away lowers the strike of the put option which gives the treasurer greater opportunity to profit from any fall in the pound without sacrificing the level of protection. On a net basis his protection is at $1.5250 ($1.5200 + $0.0050)

Strategy 11: Buy a $1.52 call option for 4.5 cents.
Write a $1.43 put option for 5 cents.

Comments: In this example the fence is put on for a small credit of 0.5 cents. This gives him the same call strike as with Strategy 10, but the put strike is higher, giving him less profit opportunity. Protection starts at $1.5150 ($1.5200 − $0.0050). The strategy has the advantage that in stable conditions it will actually earn some extra income for the treasurer by the net amount of the premium received.

Strategy 12: Buy a $1.55 call option for 3.5 cents.
Write a $1.46 put option for 7 cents.
Buy a $1.36 put option for 3.5 cents.

Comments: This strategy is effectively a three-legged zero cost fence. As in any normal fence, upside protection is maintained by the $1.55 call, and the treasurer is committed to buy sterling at $1.46 because of the short $1.46 put option. But the long $1.36 put option also allows him to benefit (to some extent) from any large-scale fall in sterling. For example, if sterling rallies to $1.75, the $1.55 call gives him the right to buy sterling at this level. Between $1.46 and $1.55 there are no rights or obligations; the treasurer buys sterling at the spot rate in the market. Between $1.46 and $1.36, he is assigned on the $1.46 put (buys pounds at $1.46). But if sterling falls to $1.25 the treasurer is able to exercise or sell back the $1.36 put which he owns and therefore to recover some of the downside move; the $1.36 put unlocks the position so that he can be protected against a rally in sterling and can still benefit in the event of a collapse. With spot at $1.25 his net purchase rate becomes $1.35 because his 10 cents loss ($1.46–$1.36) has to be offset against his eventual purchase rate.

In fact, the exposure profile of a three-legged fence is very similar to the simple strategy of buying a call option (upside protection and the opportunity – less the premium cost – to make windfall profits on any sell-off in sterling). Indeed, a $1.46 call option would cost only 7.5 cents instead of the maximum 10 cents loss for the three-legged fence. So what are the advantages? They are as follows:

1. With the fence strategy the position is constructed at zero cost; if sterling remains above $1.46 there is no obligation on behalf of the hedger and therefore no premium cost. The call option premium, by contrast, has to be paid up-front; not only does this cost have to be funded for the whole twelve-month period but if sterling fell to around $1.46, which is after all the forward outright, there would be no return from the option position. Secondly, if sterling fell marginally, say to $1.44, the net cost in one year for the fence would only be 2 cents ($1.46 – $1.44) as against the full 7.5 cent premium cost for the $1.46 call option (which, of course, has already been paid). The outright call option premium will always be cheaper than the potential cost of the three-legged fence; but in more stable conditions the fence provides better protection (a lower break-even rate) with the chance that the protection itself will be 'free'; see Table 6.2.

Strategy 13(a): Buy a $1.56 call option on full amount for 3 cents.
    Write a $1.45 put on 50 per cent of amount for 6 cents.

    13(b): Buy a $1.56 call option on full amount for 3 cents.
    Write a $1.50 put on 33 per cent of amount for 9 cents.

Sometimes known as an 'offset', this strategy, another form of a zero cost fence, gives full protection against any rally in sterling above the call strike price ($1.56) but allows the treasurer some profit potential on any

Table 6.2. Net purchase rate achieved on expiry: call option and three-legged fence.

	Spot rate on expiry						
	$1.25	$1.35	$1.45	$1.50	$1.55	$1.65	$1.75
Call purchase ($1.46 strike for 7.5 cents)	$1.325	$1.425	$1.525	$1.535	$1.535	$1.535	$1.535
Fence (3 legs)	$1.35	$1.45	$1.46	$1.50	$1.55	$1.55	$1.55

decline below the lower strike, either on 50 per cent of his position at
$1.45 (a), or on 66 per cent of his position at $1.50 (b).

The results of all the strategies mentioned to date are given in Table
6.3; this assumes that the treasurer needs to sell $100 MM/ buy sterling in
12 months' time and that today's spot rate is $1.50.

Currency options as packaged products

As well as offering these sorts of strategies (and more) many banks in the
OTC market will 'roll up' the currency option inside a package to be
offered to their corporate customers. Here is a limited selection:

Table 6.3. Profit and (loss) exposure: (nearest $1,000,000) versus original spot rate
($1.50).

	Spot rate on expiry				
	$1.25	$1.40	$1.50	$1.60	$1.75
Strategy 1: (unhedged)	$17 MM	$7 MM	Nil	($7 MM)	($17 MM)
Strategy 2: (hedged)	$3 MM	$3 MM	$3 MM	$3 MM	$3 MM
Strategy 3: (buy $1.50 call)	$13 MM	$3 MM	($4 MM)	($4 MM)	($4 MM)
Strategy 4: (buy $1.55 call)	$15 MM	$5 MM	($2 MM)	($6 MM)	($6 MM)
Strategy 5: (write $1.50 put)	$6 MM	$6 MM	$6 MM	($1 MM)	($11 MM)
Strategy 6: (buy spread)	$15 MM	$15 MM	($2 MM)	($4 MM)	($14 MM)
Strategy 7: (fence)	$7 MM	$7 MM	Nil	($3 MM)	($3 MM)
Strategy 8: (fence)	$9 MM	$7 MM	Nil	($7 MM)	($7 MM)
Strategy 9: (fence)	$4 MM	$4 MM	Nil	($1 MM)	($1 MM)
Strategy 10: (debit fence)	$6 MM	$6 MM	Nil	($2 MM)	($2 MM)
Strategy 11: (credit fence)	$5 MM	$5 MM	Nil	($1 MM)	($1 MM)
Strategy 12: (3-legged fence)	$10 MM	$3 MM	Nil	($3 MM)	($3 MM)
Strategy 13a: (offset)	$10 MM	$5 MM	Nil	($4 MM)	($4 MM)
Strategy 13b: (offset)	$11 MM	$4 MM	Nil	($4 MM)	($4 MM)

1. Deferred option premium

This is nothing more than a 'sweetener' in that the premium cost is paid, not up-front, but on the expiry date of the option. Of course the loss of interest on the premium amount is built into the total cost. This is no 'free lunch', therefore, but attractive nevertheless for potential users of the market unwilling for financial or perhaps tax and accounting reasons to part with the premium on day one. For example:

   A. Buy 12 months $1.50 call on sterling for 5.9 cents.
     (premium deferred until expiry date)

   B. Buy 12 months $1.50 call on sterling for 5.5 cents
     (premium payment up-front)

2. CAPO, break-forward, FXFG, Boston option etc.

The names are different but the strategy is the same; a CAPO is a combination of a forward purchase of a currency with a currency put; the treasurer buys the currency at a predetermined forward rate (not the 'true' forward rate, however) and at the same time secures an exit rate at which he can break the contract. There is no up-front premium.

   For example, with spot sterling $1.50, 12 months forward outright $1.46:

   A. Buy sterling forward at $1.55. Right to sell sterling at $1.48.
   B. Buy sterling forward at $1.51. Right to sell sterling at $1.40.

Again, there may be significant tax or accounting reasons why corporations would prefer to buy an option hidden inside the forward rate rather than buy a simple call option. For example, if the corporation has dollar receivables and a budgeted rate of $1.50 (the present spot rate) for the next 12 months, the treasurer can, by adopting strategy B, virtually guarantee this rate and, at the same time, allow for the opportunity of making windfall profits should sterling fall precipitously. Strategy A gives a less attractive forward rate but enables the treasurer to put a stop-loss on his position much closer to the market.

3. Tender-to-contract schemes

Several banks offer corporations the opportunity to cover against the currency risk in tender situations at a lower premium than for an outright option. Usually the arrangement is for the corporation to pay the option premium up-front (as with any normal option). But if the tender is lost the bank will refund a percentage (usually half) of the premium and the option will be cancelled. The trade-off for the corporation is that while the 'insurance' cost is reduced for any successful tenders the opportunity of making windfall profits should the tender be lost and the option be in-the-money is sacrificed. For example:

UK corporation tenders for contract in the United States:

Needs to cover risk of rising sterling/dollar rate (spot rate $1.50):

A. Buy $1.50 call for 5.5 cents.

B. Buy TTC $1.50 call for 5.5 cents.

Tender contract won: net option profit/loss: spot $1.75:

A. Simple call option: 19.5 cents.

B. TTC option: 19.5 cents.

Tender contract lost: net option profit/loss: spot $1.75:

A. Simple call option: 19.5 cents.

B. TTC option: 2.75 cents

4. Options on options

Sometimes known as 'compound options', the structure works in the following way. The corporation has the choice of buying a $1.50 call for 5.5 cents, or buying an option on the $1.50 call for 2.75 cents. Should he buy the compound option, and were sterling to fall, his only cost is the original 2.75 cents. But should sterling rally and the corporation wish to exercise the option he must pay the original 5.5 cents premium on top of the compound option premium of 2.75 cents. In stable to lower conditions, therefore, the compound option is cheaper; on any rally in sterling, however, the final cost is 50 per cent more than the simple call buying strategy, for example:

A. Buy sterling $1.50 call for 5.5 cents.

B. Buy option on $1.50 call option for 2.75 cents.

Total premium costs (cents) on expiry:

Strategy	Spot sterling		
	$1.30	$1.50	$1.70
A:	5.5	5.5	5.5
B:	2.75	2.75	8.25

Yield enhancement: using currency options to maximise returns and/or reduce risks

The strategies

Inevitably, the concentration of Chapters 5 and 6 on using currency options to avoid risk has led to a bias towards the corporate treasurer and his exposures rather than the international investor. In reality the distinction between the treasurer and the investor, as between the hedger and the trader, is blurred; many corporate treasurers write options and many international fund managers buy options, and the strategies outlined previously, particularly in Chapter 6, may apply to the investment manager and the corporate treasurer alike. However, if both camps will write as well as buy options the main distinguishing feature is in that of emphasis: both the treasurer and the investor use currency options to reduce risk, but the investor is also in the business of achieving a return. The purpose of this chapter is to demonstrate some of the option strategies available designed to enhance the return on a foreign investment and/or to reduce the level of currency risk.

Certainly the currency risk is significant; the investor who moves overseas is effectively going long of the currency in which he invests. Switching out of US into Canadian Treasury bills, or from Wall Street into UK equities, is creating, in addition to the interest rate or stock market risk, a foreign exchange exposure – the investor is long, respectively, of the Canadian dollar or of sterling versus the US dollar. Similarly, the US international fund manager who buys Japanese bonds is risking a fall in the yen as well as an increase in Japanese interest rates.

Take the example of a US dollar based investor who buys a three month sterling time deposit to take advantage of the higher yield:

Strategy 1:
a. Sell US dollars/buy sterling spot at $1.60.
b. Buy sterling three months' time deposit yielding 9.5 per cent.

Horizon returns:[1] unhedged
Spot rate

	$1.50	$1.55	$1.60	$1.65	$1.70
% yield	−15.5	−3.0	9.5	22	34.5

Any yield pick-up will be quickly eroded on any adverse currency movement; any rally in the pound will provide windfall profits.

Forward hedge

Any attempt to hedge this risk by selling sterling in the forward foreign exchange market, however, is likely to be counter-productive; the yield achieved will at best match, but more likely underperform the simple strategy of buying US dollar deposits. This, of course, is the result of the arbitrage process at work in the foreign exchange market which ensures that forward foreign exchange rates reflect accurately the interest differential between the two respective currencies.

Strategy 2: forward hedge
a. Sell US dollars/buy sterling spot at $1.60.
b. Buy sterling three months time deposit yielding 9.5 per cent.
c. Sell sterling forward at $1.5875.

Horizon returns: hedged
Spot

	$1.50	$1.55	$1.60	$1.65	$1.70
% yield	6.3	6.3	6.3	6.3	6.3

Put buying

The option strategy, therefore, would seem to have some appeal, particularly if the interest rate differential can in some way be locked in. Unfortunately, the arbitrage process in the currency options market ensures that the cost of the premium – in this case the sterling put premium – will also reflect the same interest rate differential. In a correctly priced option market it is simply not possible to lock in a higher return by investing in a higher yielding currency and buying a currency put.

Strategy 3: buy at-the-money put (see Fig. 7.1)
a. Sell US dollars/buy sterling spot at $1.60.
b. Buy sterling three months time deposit yielding 9.5 per cent.
c. Buy sterling $1.60 put for 4.4 cents.

[1] All returns annualised.

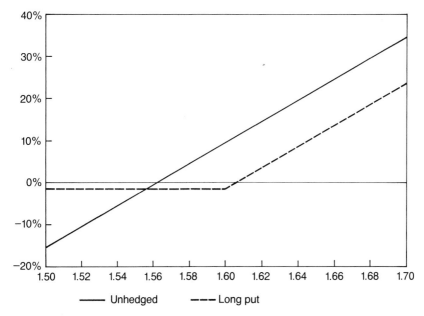

Fig. 7.1   Buy sterling at-the-money put.

Horizon returns: buy put

Spot	$1.50	$1.55	$1.60	$1.65	$1.70
% yield	−1.50	−1.50	−1.50	11	23.5

On expiration, if the spot is lower than $1.60, exercise the put. If the spot is higher than $1.60, let the option expire unexercised and sell sterling/buy US dollars at the prevailing spot rate. Seen in insurance terms the higher the strike the better the protection; but at the same time the lower will be the standstill return and the higher the pound has to move to show any improvement over the original US dollar yield. Alternatively, it may be preferable to buy the out-of-the-money option as 'disaster insurance'.

Strategy 4: buy out-of-the-money put (see Fig. 7.2)
a. Sell US dollars/buy sterling spot at $1.60.
b. Buy sterling three months time deposit yielding 9.5 per cent.
c. Buy sterling $1.55 put for 2.1 cents.

Horizon returns: buy put

	$1.50	$1.55	$1.60	$1.65	$1.70
% yield	−8.25	−8.25	4.25	16.75	29.25

Thus the $1.60 put gives good downside protection but the return is very poor without a strong rally in sterling; the $1.55 put provides a better

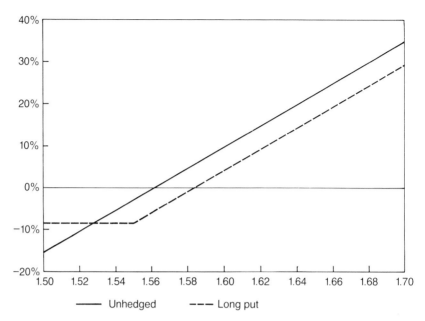

Fig. 7.2   Buy sterling out-of-the-money put.

standstill return (although still lower than could be achieved by simply buying US dollar deposits); a sterling rally will result in a better perform-ance than with the at-the-money put but the losses will be greater on any downturn. In conclusion, the strategy of buying currency puts has little to recommend it for the purposes of cross-currency trading.

A similar end result applies to any high yielding currency; the cost of the insurance, the put premium, negates to a very large extent the effectiveness of the strategy. With a six month Australian dollar deposit yielding 15.5 per cent a put option struck at the spot rate ($0.70) would cost approximately 2 cents. The returns on the strategy of investing in Australian dollar deposits and buying an out-of-the-money put option would look as follows:

a. Sell US dollars/buy Australian dollars spot at $0.70.
b. Buy Australian dollars three months time deposit yielding 15.5 per cent.

Horizon returns: unhedged (see Fig. 7.3)

Spot $ Australian	0.64	0.66	0.68	0.70	0.72	0.74	0.76
% yield	−19	−7.3	4	15.5	27	38	50

By comparison, the returns on a fully hedged basis would be as follows:

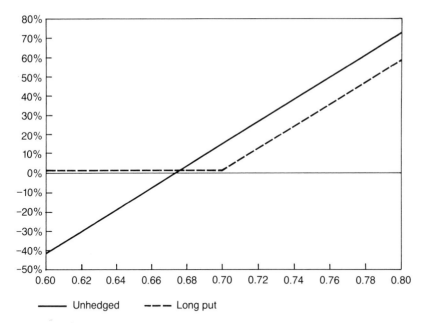

Fig. 7.3   Buy Australian dollar put.

Horizon returns: hedged
Spot $ Australian

	0.66	0.68	0.70	0.72	0.74
% yield	6.3	6.3	6.3	6.3	6.3

Horizon returns: buy $0.70 put for $.025
Spot $ Australian

	0.62	0.64	0.66	0.68	0.70	0.72	0.74	0.76
% yield	1.2%	1.2%	1.2%	1.2%	1.2%	12.6%	24%	35.5%

It can be safely assumed that, given an efficient option market, it is not possible to lock in the yield on a higher yielding instrument and hedge the currency risk by buying a put option.

Call writing

As an alternative to buying puts the investor might well look at the strategy of writing currency call options. Such a combination, used extensively in the stock option market, is akin to writing insurance; the premium received increases the standstill return and at the same time gives some downside protection in the event of a currency decline. Ideally a European style option should be written because the convenience of not having the option exercised early – of having the currency called away before the maturity of the deposit – far outweighs the penalty of the reduced premium for the European as against the American style sterling call option.

Strategy 5: write deep-in-the-money call (see Fig. 7.4)
a. Sell US dollars/buy sterling spot at $1.60.
b. Buy sterling three months time deposit yielding 9.5 per cent.
c. Write sterling $1.50 call for 9.2 cents.

Horizon returns: sell call

Spot

	$1.45	$1.50	$1.55	$1.60	$1.65	$1.70
% Yield	−5	7.5	7.5	7.5	7.5	7.5

Writing the deep-in-the-money ($1.50) call, while not riskless, is the closest to locking in the return on a higher yielding instrument; the option will almost certainly be exercised because it is deep in-the-money, but the time premium received, albeit small, is sufficient to increase the yield to a level higher than would be available for a US dollar deposit. The risk is that the currency falls below the $1.50 strike so that the option becomes out-of-the-money and loses its protection.

If the call is exercised on expiration day the spot currency made available from the sterling time deposit is delivered to the owner of the

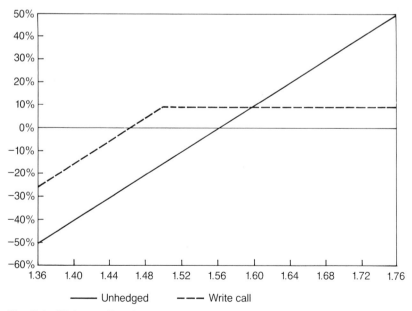

Fig. 7.4   Write sterling deep in-the-money call.

option. If the option is not exercised, the currency has to be sold at the spot sterling/dollar rate in the market.

Strategy 6: write at-the-money call (see Fig. 7.5)
a. Sell US dollars/buy sterling spot at $1.60.
b. Buy sterling three months time deposit yielding 9.5 per cent.
c. Write sterling $1.60 call for 2.8 cents.

Horizon returns: sell call

Spot	$1.45	$1.50	$1.55	$1.60	$1.65	$1.70
% yield	−21	−8.5	4.0	16.5	16.5	16.5

Writing the $1.60 call gives a higher standstill return than writing the deep-in-the-money option because the time premium is greater; the 'cushion' of protection against any fall in sterling, however, is correspondingly less. Therefore, the strategy works best in stable conditions.

Strategy 7: write out-of-the-money call (see Fig. 7.6)
a. Sell US dollars/buy sterling spot at $1.60.
b. Buy sterling three months time deposit yielding 9.5 per cent.
c. Write sterling $1.65 call for 1.2 cents.

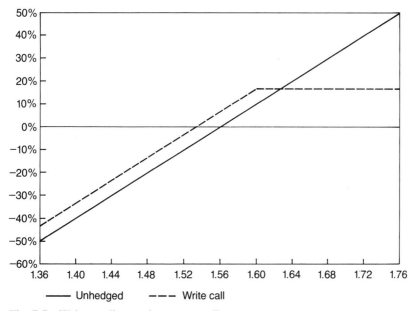

Fig. 7.5   Write sterling at-the-money call.

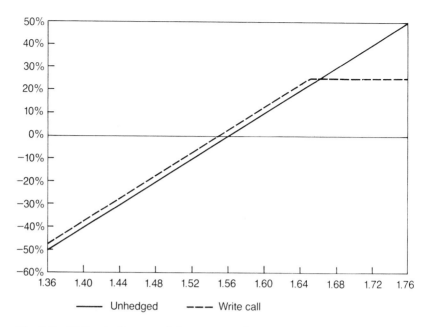

Fig. 7.6   Write sterling out-of-the-money call.

Horizon returns: sell call
Spot

	$1.45	$1.50	$1.55	$1.60	$1.65	$1.70
% yield	−25	−12.5	0	12.5	25	25

The strategy of writing an out-of-the-money call option is fundamentally different; here the investor has to be at least moderately bullish on the currency because the protection afforded by the option premium received is far too small to act as any realistic cushion against a drop in sterling. The strategy aims to profit from a high deposit yield, from a rally in the currency, and from the option premium income. The maximum return available following a rally in sterling – the so-called 'if exercised return', is greater than the standstill return by the amount the option strike is out-of-the-money. This strategy would be best employed given a reasonably bullish view of sterling.

It is questionable, however, if a covered call strategy should be used at all given a very bullish view of the pound. Selling the call option automatically limits the profit potential of the trade, the downside cushion is very small on an out-of-the-money option, and the returns available from an unhedged position are the greatest (given a strong rally).

The main purpose of writing currency call options is to increase the return on an investment. But in highly volatile conditions some upside potential can be sacrificed in order to provide a larger downside cushion. This can be achieved by writing in-the-money options. By contrast, an investor with a higher tolerance of risk, or with a more bullish view of the currency, could write out-of-the-money options; this will allow greater potential profits but with less downside protection.

The return on any high-yielding 'paper' can be increased through the short call hedge. With Australian dollars, for example:

a. Sell US dollars/buy Australian dollars spot at $0.70.
b. Buy three month Australian dollar time deposit yielding 15.5 per cent.
c. Write $0.70 three month European call for $0.0075.

Horizon returns: short call (see Fig. 7.7)

Spot Australian dollar

	0.62	0.64	0.66	0.68	0.70	0.72	0.74	0.76
% yield	−26	−15	−3	8.3	20	20	20	20

Here the at-the-money call increases the standstill return from 15.5 per cent to 20 per cent; the premium received from writing the call gives the investor a downside cushion which protects the position effectively even given a 2 cent or 2.85 per cent fall in the currency. The trade-off of such a

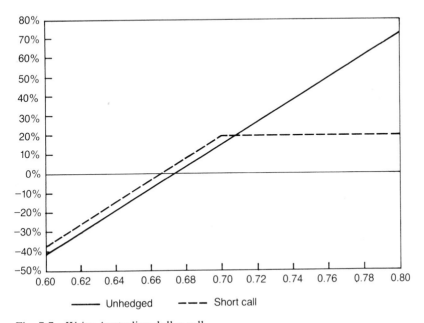

Fig. 7.7   Write Australian dollar call.

strategy is that windfall profits resulting from a rally in the Australian dollar are eliminated above the strike level at which the call is written.

However, although the call writing strategy provides a cushion against a fall in the currency, any substantial decline will still leave the position looking very vulnerable, and on a strong rally the covered write under-performs by a distance the simple unhedged position. Such a strategy, therefore, works best in an environment of stable to rising foreign exchange rates. In highly volatile conditions the risks are still substantial, however.

As a way of reducing the downside risk the concept of writing calls and buying puts, the fence trade, works as effectively for cross-currency traders as for the corporate treasurer. The strategy has the advantage that by adjusting the strikes of the calls and puts, the risk/return character-istics of the investment can be more precisely defined so as to mirror the investor's view of the market. The fence can be constructed for a credit, for a debit, or for zero cost.

Strategy 8: fence (write call/buy put)
a. Sell US dollars/buy sterling spot at $1.60.
b. Buy sterling three months' time deposit yielding 9.5 per cent.
c. Write sterling $1.60 call for 2.8 cents
d. Buy sterling $1.55 put for 2.1 cents.

Horizon returns: credit fence (see Fig. 7.8)
Spot

	$1.50	$1.55	$1.60	$1.65	$1.70
% yield	−1.25	−1.25	11.25	11.25	11.25

The investor has the right to sell sterling at $1.55 and is committed to sell sterling at $1.60. At expiration, if the spot is above $1.60 the sterling call will be exercised and the currency automatically sold out at this level; therefore maximum returns, by definition, will be at the $1.60 level. Should sterling be below $1.55, the put should be exercised, allowing the investor to sell his proceeds at this level whatever the spot rate happens to be in the market. In between $1.55 and $1.60 there is no obligation or right from the investor's point of view; he will consequently sell sterling at the prevailing spot rate.

Strategy 9: fence (write call/buy put)
a. Sell US dollars/buy sterling spot at $1.60.
b. Buy sterling three months' time deposit yielding 9.5 per cent.
c. Write sterling $1.65 call for 1.2 cents
d. Buy sterling $1.55 put for 2.1 cents.

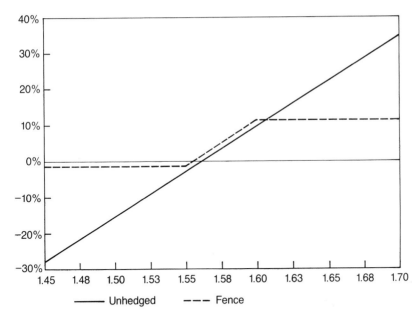

Fig. 7.8   Credit 'fence': sterling.

Horizon returns: debit fence (see Fig. 7.9)

Spot	$1.50	$1.55	$1.60	$1.65	$1.70
% yield	−5.25	−5.25	7.25	19.25	19.25

The investor has the right to sell sterling at $1.55 and the commitment to sell sterling at $1.65. Consequently, the strategy gives the investor the opportunity of greater profits on any sterling rally, but with the trade-off of larger losses on any decline.

The combination possibilities involving calls and puts are virtually unlimited. One variation is where another 'leg' is added to the fence to allow the investor the chance of making large windfall profits on any substantial rally; this overcomes the major disadvantage of a fence where upside gains are limited by the strike level of the short call option. The trade-off is that, whereas upside profits are theoretically unlimited, the standstill returns are lower than with a conventional fence.

Strategy 10: three-legged fence
a. Sell US dollars/buy sterling spot at $1.60.
b. Buy sterling three months' time deposit yielding 9.5 per cent.
c. Buy sterling $1.55 put for 2.1 cents
d. Write sterling $1.60 call for 2.8 cents.
e. Buy $1.65 sterling call for 1.4 cents

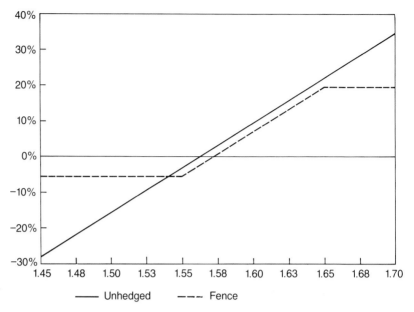

Fig. 7.9   Debit 'fence': sterling.

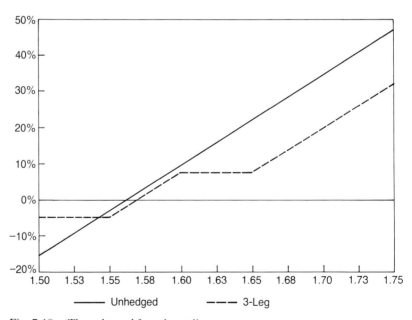

Fig. 7.10   'Three-legged fence': sterling.

Horizon returns: three-legged fence (see Fig. 7.10)

	$1.50	$1.55	$1.60	$1.65	$1.70
% yield	−4.75	−4.75	7.75	7.75	20.5

Action on expiration day:

Spot $1.55 or below: exercise $1.55 put and delivery sterling at $1.55.

Spot $1.55 – $1.60: Sell sterling at prevailing spot rate.

Spot $1.60 – $1.65: $1.60 call exercised (therefore deliver sterling at $1.60).

Spot $1.65 and above: allow $1.60 call to be exercised (therefore deliver sterling at $1.60) and sell back $1.65 call to the market for its intrinsic value.

Alternatively, if the investor feels that sterling will remain stable over the horizon period he can maximise his return by constructing a 'butterfly' hedge; here two at-the-money calls are written and out-of-the-money puts and calls purchased in order to prevent losses on any large sterling fall or rally.

Strategy 11: butterfly hedge (see Fig. 7.11)
a. Sell US dollars/buy sterling spot at $1.60.
b. Buy sterling three month time deposit yielding 9.5 per cent.
c. Buy sterling $1.55 put for 2.1 cents
d. Write two sterling $1.60 calls for 5.6 cents.
e. Buy $1.65 sterling call for 1.4 cents.

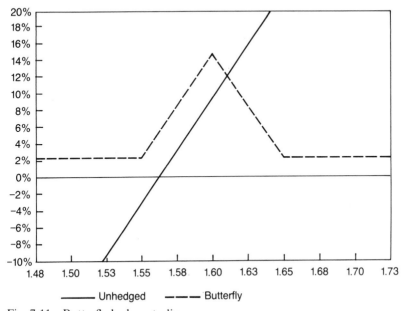

Fig. 7.11   Butterfly hedge: sterling.

Horizon returns: butterfly hedge
Spot

	$1.50	$1.55	$1.60	$1.65	$1.70
% yield	2.25	2.25	14.75	2.25	2.25

Action on expiration day:

Spot $1.55 or below: exercise put and deliver sterling at $1.55.

Spot $1.55 – $1.60: Sell sterling at the prevailing spot rate.

Spot $1.60 – $1.65: Buy back one $1.60 call option for maximum loss of 5 cents, allow other $1.60 call to be assigned (therefore deliver sterling at $1.60).

Spot $1.65 and above: lose 5 cents on one $1.60 call ($1.65 – $1.60) and allow other $1.60 call to be assigned (therefore deliver sterling at $1.60).

The whole strategy of US dollar based investors buying higher yielding 'paper' denominated in foreign currencies and reducing the currency risk or maximising the return through the use of currency options, can be turned on its head; it is equally possible for a sterling based investor, for example, to buy a US dollar deposit and hedge some of the currency risk through the option market.

Strategy 12: sterling based investor buys US dollar deposit
a. Sell sterling/buy US dollars spot at $1.60.
b. Buy three months US dollar deposit yielding 6.4 per cent.
c. Write sterling $1.60 put for 4 cents.

Horizon returns: put write
Spot

	$1.50	$1.55	$1.60	$1.65	$1.70
% yield	16.4	16.4	16.4	3.9	−8.6

Hedging fixed income investments

For the international fixed income investor the opening up of capital and money markets around the world has led to the development of new strategies designed to exploit cross-border yield differentials. Whereas the existence of efficient Eurocurrency deposit and spot and forward foreign exchange markets has meant that short- to medium-term cross-currency financing on a fully hedged basis is usually a zero-sum game, inefficiencies do indeed occur from time to time in the international bond markets. In such circumstances it is possible to capture yield pick-ups even after hedging the currency risk. In January 1985, for example, it was possible to switch out of three year US Treasury bonds into three year UK gilts and pick up over 180 basis points in yield after hedging the principal and future coupon payments in the forward foreign exchange markets. Similarly, an investment in three year West German government bonds, fully hedged, yielded a 60 basis point advantage over the equivalent US Treasuries. In December 1985, gilts in the 3 – 5 year maturity area were yielding about 60 basis points over US Treasuries, again on a fully hedged basis.[2]

But even if such arbitrage opportunities occur only infrequently, the concept of investing in higher-yielding foreign fixed income markets has much to be said for it. For one, question marks about the credit-ratings of several high-yielding 'junk bond' issuers in the aftermath of various insider-dealing scandals recently has undermined confidence in the market. With government bond yields in the UK, Canada, Australia, and New Zealand offering yield advantages of anything from 200 to 1,000 basis points over comparable US Treasuries, the strategy of swapping the credit risk of 'junk bonds' for the currency risk associated with investing in foreign government bonds can be attractive. Not only are most foreign government bond markets more liquid than the 'junk bond' market, (this is particularly the case in a period when credit scares can threaten to undermine the whole structure of the market), but hedging tools for coping with foreign exchange risk are liquid and highly developed; there is no effective means of hedging the credit risk of an individual bond.

Table 5.1 (showing international bond market performance) well illustrates the advantages of investing in foreign currency bonds during periods of US dollar weakness. Through the use of the forward foreign exchange market and the currency option market, the international investor has at his disposal a virtually unlimited number of strategy variations with which to hedge or control the risk of the resulting currency exposures.

Take the example of a US dollar based investor who moves into the UK gilt market:

Buying gilts and hedging the currency risk.
Trade date: 20/3/87
UK Treasury 11.75% 20/3/07:
Price £126.12. Yield 8.86%. Dividend date: 22/7/87.
Spot sterling/dollar $1.60.
22/7/87 Forward rate: $1.5840

Investment strategy:
a. Sell US dollars/buy sterling spot at $1.60.
b. Buy gilt.

[2] Of course, one of the reasons that such opportunities did, and still do, exist is that the arbitrage is not fully reflecting the credit risk in the long-dated forward foreign exchange market. In other words, the process of buying gilts and selling sterling three years forward creates not a proxy US Treasury bond but a proxy Eurodollar bond, with a higher yield than the Treasury market reflecting the higher credit risk in the forward market.

Returns (non-annualised) on dividend date:
Currency hedging strategy:

A. Unhedged

Ex. Rate:	Gilt Yield 8.00	8.25	8.50	8.75	9.00	9.25	9.50
1.75	20.33	18.01	15.76	13.58	11.45	9.39	7.39
1.70	16.89	14.64	12.45	10.33	8.27	6.27	4.32
1.65	13.45	11.27	9.15	7.09	5.09	3.14	1.26
1.60	10.01	7.89	5.84	3.84	1.90	0.02	−1.81
1.55	6.58	4.52	2.53	0.60	−1.28	−3.11	−4.88
1.50	3.14	1.15	−0.78	−2.65	−4.47	−6.23	−7.95
1.45	−0.30	−2.22	−4.08	−5.89	−7.65	−9.36	−11.02

B. Forward hedge

Ex. Rate:	Gilt Yield 8.00	8.25	8.50	8.75	9.00	9.25	9.50
1.75	9.95	7.63	5.39	3.20	1.08	−0.98	−2.98
1.70	9.64	7.39	5.20	3.08	1.02	−0.98	−2.93
1.65	9.33	7.14	5.02	2.96	0.96	−0.98	−2.87
1.60	9.01	6.89	4.84	2.84	0.90	−0.98	−2.81
1.55	8.70	6.65	4.66	2.72	0.84	−0.98	−2.76
1.50	8.39	6.40	4.47	2.60	0.78	−0.98	−2.70
1.45	8.07	6.15	4.29	2.48	0.72	−0.98	−2.64

C. Buy at-the-money sterling put for 4.6 cents

Ex. Rate:	Gilt Yield 8.00	8.25	8.50	8.75	9.00	9.25	9.50
1.75	16.96	14.71	12.53	10.40	8.34	6.34	4.39
1.70	13.62	11.43	9.31	7.25	5.24	3.30	1.41
1.65	10.28	8.16	6.10	4.09	2.15	0.26	−1.57
1.60	6.94	4.88	2.88	0.94	−0.95	−2.78	−4.56
1.55	6.63	4.64	2.70	0.82	−1.00	−2.78	−4.50
1.50	6.33	4.40	2.53	0.71	−1.06	−2.78	−4.45
1.45	6.03	4.16	2.35	0.59	−1.12	−2.78	−4.39

D. Buy out-of-the-money ($1.55) put for 2.5 cents

Ex. Rate:	Gilt Yield 8.00	8.25	8.50	8.75	9.00	9.25	9.50
1.75	18.48	16.19	13.98	11.83	9.74	7.71	5.74
1.70	15.09	12.87	10.72	8.63	6.60	4.63	2.72
1.65	11.71	9.55	7.47	5.44	3.47	1.56	−0.30
1.60	8.32	6.23	4.21	2.24	0.33	−1.52	−3.32
1.55	4.94	2.92	0.95	−0.95	−2.80	−4.60	−6.34
1.50	4.63	2.67	0.77	−1.07	−2.86	−4.60	−6.29
1.45	4.32	2.43	0.59	−1.19	−2.92	−4.60	−6.23

E. Buy far out-of-the-money ($1.50) put for 1 cent

Ex. Rate:	Gilt Yield 8.00	8.25	8.50	8.75	9.00	9.25	9.50
1.75	19.58	17.28	15.04	12.87	10.76	8.71	6.72
1.70	16.16	13.93	11.75	9.65	7.60	5.61	3.68
1.65	12.75	10.58	8.47	6.42	4.43	2.50	0.63
1.60	9.33	7.22	5.18	3.20	1.27	−0.60	−2.42
1.55	5.91	3.87	1.89	−0.03	−1.90	−3.71	−5.47

| 1.50 | 2.50 | 0.52 | −1.39 | −3.25 | −5.06 | −6.82 | −8.52 |
| 1.45 | 2.19 | 0.28 | −1.57 | −3.37 | −5.12 | −6.82 | −8.47 |

F. Write deep in-the-money ($1.50) call for 9 cents

Gilt Yield

Ex. Rate:	8.00	8.25	8.50	8.75	9.00	9.25	9.50
1.75	10.94	8.49	6.10	3.79	1.54	−0.64	−2.76
1.70	10.61	8.23	5.91	3.66	1.48	−0.64	−2.70
1.65	10.28	7.96	5.72	3.53	1.41	−0.64	−2.64
1.60	9.95	7.70	5.52	3.41	1.35	−0.64	−2.58
1.55	9.62	7.44	5.33	3.28	1.29	−0.65	−2.52
1.50	9.28	7.18	5.14	3.15	1.23	−0.65	−2.46
1.45	5.64	3.61	1.63	−0.29	−2.15	−3.96	−5.71

G. Write in-the-money ($1.55) call for 5.2 cents

Gilt Yield

Ex. Rate:	8.00	8.25	8.50	8.75	9.00	9.25	9.50
1.75	11.45	9.05	6.73	4.47	2.28	0.15	−1.92
1.70	11.13	8.80	6.54	4.35	2.22	0.15	−1.86
1.65	10.80	8.54	6.35	4.22	2.16	0.15	−1.80
1.60	10.48	8.29	6.16	4.10	2.09	0.15	−1.75
1.55	10.16	8.03	5.97	3.97	2.03	0.15	−1.69
1.50	6.60	4.55	2.56	0.62	−1.26	−3.08	−4.86
1.45	3.05	1.06	−0.86	−2.73	−4.55	−6.32	−8.03

H. Write at-the-money ($1.60) call for 2.6 cents

Gilt Yield

Ex. Rate:	8.00	8.25	8.50	8.75	9.00	9.25	9.50
1.75	12.78	10.43	8.14	5.92	3.77	1.67	−0.36
1.70	12.47	10.18	7.96	5.80	3.70	1.67	−0.31
1.65	12.15	9.93	7.77	5.68	3.64	1.67	−0.25
1.60	11.83	9.68	7.59	5.56	3.58	1.67	−0.19
1.55	8.34	6.25	4.22	2.26	0.35	−1.51	−3.31
1.50	4.84	2.82	0.86	−1.04	−2.89	−4.69	−6.43
1.45	1.35	−0.61	−2.50	−4.34	−6.13	−7.86	−9.55

I. Write out-of-the-money ($1.65) call for 1.1 cents

Gilt Yield

Ex. Rate:	8.00	8.25	8.50	8.75	9.00	9.25	9.50
1.75	14.87	12.53	10.27	8.07	5.93	3.86	1.84
1.70	14.55	12.29	10.08	7.95	5.87	3.86	1.90
1.65	14.24	12.04	9.90	7.83	5.81	3.86	1.96
1.60	10.78	8.64	6.57	4.56	2.61	0.71	−1.13
1.55	7.31	5.25	3.24	1.29	−0.60	−2.44	−4.22
1.50	3.85	1.85	−0.09	−1.98	−3.81	−5.59	−7.31
1.45	0.39	−1.54	−3.42	−5.24	−7.01	−8.73	−10.40

J. 'Fence': zero cost
Write sterling $1.60 call for 2.6 cents
Buy sterling $1.55 put for 2.6 cents

Gilt Yield

Ex. Rate:	8.00	8.25	8.50	8.75	9.00	9.25	9.50
1.75	10.95	8.63	6.39	4.20	2.08	0.02	−1.98
1.70	10.64	8.39	6.20	4.08	2.02	0.02	−1.93
1.65	10.33	8.14	6.02	3.96	1.96	0.02	−1.87
1.60	10.01	7.89	5.84	3.84	1.90	0.02	−1.81

1.55	6.58	4.52	2.53	0.60	−1.28	−3.11	−4.88
1.50	6.26	4.28	2.35	0.48	−1.34	−3.11	−4.82
1.45	5.95	4.03	2.17	0.36	−1.40	−3.11	−4.77

K. Debit 'fence':
Write $1.65 sterling call for 1.1 cents
Buy $1.55 put for 2.5 cents

Gilt Yield

Ex. Rate:	8.00	8.25	8.50	8.75	9.00	9.25	9.50
1.75	9.85	7.56	5.33	3.17	1.07	−0.97	−2.95
1.70	9.54	7.32	5.15	3.05	1.01	−0.97	−2.90
1.65	9.23	7.07	4.97	2.93	0.95	−0.97	−2.84
1.60	8.92	6.83	4.79	2.81	0.89	−0.97	−2.79
1.55	5.52	3.49	1.52	−0.40	−2.26	−4.07	−5.82
1.50	2.12	0.15	−1.76	−3.61	−5.41	−7.16	−8.86
1.45	1.81	−0.09	−1.94	−3.73	−5.47	−7.16	−8.81

L. Credit 'fence'
Write sterling $1.60 call for 2.6 cents
Buy sterling $1.50 put for 1 cent

Gilt Yield

Ex. Rate:	8.00	8.25	8.50	8.75	9.00	9.25	9.50
1.75	15.01	12.68	10.41	8.20	6.07	3.99	1.97
1.70	14.70	12.43	10.22	8.08	6.01	3.99	2.03
1.65	14.38	12.18	10.04	7.96	5.95	3.99	2.08
1.60	10.91	8.78	6.70	4.69	2.74	0.84	−1.01
1.55	7.45	5.38	3.37	1.42	−0.47	−2.32	−4.10
1.50	7.13	5.13	3.19	1.30	−0.53	−2.32	−4.05
1.45	6.82	4.88	3.00	1.18	−0.59	−2.32	−3.99

The effects of these strategies are shown in Figs 7.12 – 7.15.

In conclusion, it can be seen that the permutations open to the international investor are virtually limitless. By varying the strikes and combinations of strategies, any number of ways of adjusting the risk/reward scenario can be created. Where the currency bond option market is also liquid and efficient, bond option strategies can be combined with currency option strategies as a method of hedging the risk on the bond as well as the currency risk. A dual covered write, selling a currency call and a currency bond call, is one possibility. Another permutation would be to construct a currency fence to lock in the risk and return on the foreign exchange market, and at the same time using a bond fence to adjust the price exposure risk on the bond position.

Two further points need to be made, however:

1. Apart from exceptional circumstances, there is no strategy available which automatically can lock in the higher return on a foreign investment; the multiplicity of choice in terms of hedging strategies open to the investor is only a means of reducing the risk or maximising the return. No strategy, however complex, can eliminate risk and at the same time ensure a higher return.

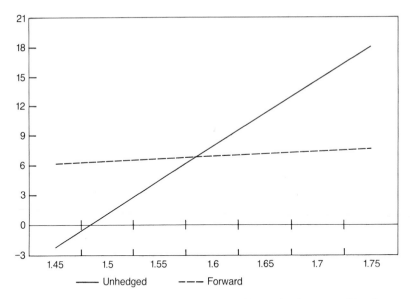

Fig. 7.12   Invest in UK gilts: currency hedged/unhedged returns. (Total return versus exchange rate – assuming gilt yields move 8.25%.)

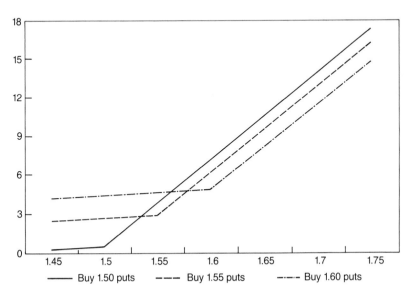

Fig. 7.13   Invest in UK gilts: buy sterling puts. (Total return versus exchange rate – assuming gilt yields move 8.25%.)

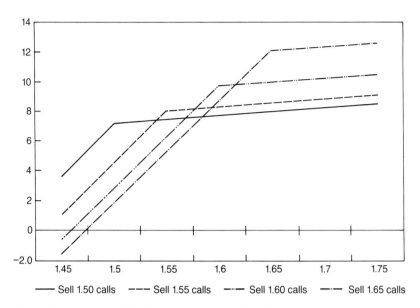

Fig. 7.14   Invest in UK gilts: write sterling calls. (Total return versus exchange rate – assuming gilt yields move 8.25%.)

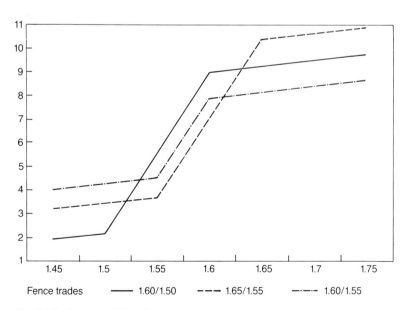

Fig. 7.15   Invest in UK gilts: fence hedge. (Total return versus exchange rate – assuming 8.25% gilt yields.)

2. It should not be assumed that option strategies, particularly covered call writing, should simply be left to mature with time. Active management of the position is important in order to increase the potential return on the investment. On the one level, if a currency call option is written against a foreign currency bond position and both the bond and the currency lose value quickly, the best strategy may well be to cut losses and close the whole position out. At the other extreme, a short currency call option may be a great liability should the currency itself rally sharply through the strike level; the best strategy again may be to cut the option position, to buy back the call at a loss in anticipation of making substantially higher profits on the bond position. Alternatively, the investor should look at ways of adjusting his option positions so as to cover himself against a downside move, or to increase his return given a rally in the currency. At all events, the option hedge should not be left idle but monitored and if necessary managed on a regular basis.

CHAPTER 8

Covered call writing: managing the option hedge

Strategies in a falling currency market

Should the underlying currency decline in price during the lifetime of the investment the call option will also fall in value. This fall in the premium will be greater the longer it takes for the currency itself to fall; in other words, time decay works in the option writer's favour. By rolling down with the market, that is buying back the short call for a profit and selling a new call option to match the maturity of the investment, the option writer hopes to increase his overall returns. The further the option moves away from the money the less impact will the movement in the spot rate have on the option's value; by covering the out-of-the-money option and replacing the position with a nearer to the money strike the investor is squeezing more time premium out of the covered call strategy. The overall returns will be higher, therefore, than for the simple, unadjusted, option writing position.

Returning to the original example of the sterling time deposit investment (Strategy 1):

a. Sell US dollars/buy sterling spot at $1.60.
b. Buy sterling three months time deposit yielding 9.5 per cent.

Horizon returns: unhedged

	$1.50	$1.55	$1.60	$1.65	$1.70
% yield	−15.5	−3.0	9.5	22	34.5

In order to increase the yield in a stable market the $1.60 (at-the-money) call is written (Strategy 6).

Write sterling three months $1.60 call for 2.8 cents.

Horizon returns: covered call write

	$1.45	$1.50	$1.55	$1.60	$1.65	$1.70
% yield	−21	−8.5	4.0	16.5	16.5	16.5

However, instead of analysing horizon returns, we look at the position after 45 days and assume that the spot rate had declined to $1.55, the $1.60 call option would now be five cents out-of-the-money and worth only 0.5 cents approximately. At the same time, the $1.55 call option expiring in 45 days, that is the same expiration date of the original option and the value date of the time deposit, is bid 2 cents. Given this scenario, the call writer might buy back his $1.60 call option for a profit of 2.3 cents (2.8 cents − 0.5 cents) and write the 'new' at-the-money $1.55 call and receive a further 2 cents. The horizon returns of the whole strategy would subsequently look as follows on day 90, expiration day:

Day 1: spot $1.60
Write three months $1.60 call for 2.8 cents.

Day 45: spot $1.55
Buy back $1.60 call for 0.5 cents
Write 45 day $1.55 call for 2 cents.

Day 90: horizon returns

	$1.45	$1.50	$1.55	$1.60	$1.65	$1.70
% yield	−17.3	−4.8	7.8	7.8	7.8	7.8

In an environment of falling foreign exchange rates the active strategy of rolling down outperforms the passive strategy of sitting on the original short option position. However, any subsequent rally in sterling will reduce the profitability of the trade because the lower strike of the new option ($1.55) limits any further upside potential.

Strategies in a rising currency market

When the spot currency rises, the original short at-the-money call option is now in-the-money. Buying back the short call and replacing it with a 'new' at-the-money call for the same expiry allows the underlying investment to retain greater profit potential while at the same time maintaining a defensive 'cushion' against a subsequent downturn in the market.

Day 1: spot $1.60
Write three months $1.60 call for 2.8 cents.

Day 45: spot $1.65
Buy back $1.60 call for 5.2 cents.
Write 45 day $1.65 call for 2 cents.

Day 90: horizon returns

	$1.45	$1.50	$1.55	$1.60	$1.65	$1.70
% yield	−29	−16.5	−4	8.5	21	21

In this situation the strategy of rolling up works well as long as sterling continues to improve (or at least hold its own); it outperforms the original 'write and hold' strategy in such circumstances but underperforms should the pound fall back to the $1.60 level or below.

When to adjust the hedge

Of course, the timing and frequency of the rolls as well as the strike selection is not an arbitrary process. The investor could use technical analysis as a guide, rolling down into a lower strike – perhaps even a deep in-the-money option for defensive purposes – on a sell signal from his trading model. Alternatively, he could use the delta as a trigger mechanism for his rolls, selling at-the-money calls with deltas of about 0.5 and rolling up when the delta increases to about 0.7 and rolling down when the delta falls below 0.3:

Day 1: spot $1.60
Write $1.60 call (delta 0.45) for 2.8 cents.

Day 30: spot $1.65
Buy back $1.60 call (delta 0.70) for 5.3 cents
Write $1.65 (60 day) call (delta 0.46) for 2.4 cents.

Day 60: spot $1.69
Buy back $1.65 call (delta 0.75) for 4.2 cents
Write $1.69 (30) day call (delta 0.47) for 1.8 cents.

Day 90: horizon returns

	$1.60	$1.65	$1.70	$1.75 and above
% yield	3.25	15.75	25.75	25.75

The delta-adjusted roll-up strategy again works effectively in a rising market. Of course a sharp sell-off in sterling during the last 30 days of the strategy could leave the position vulnerable. As a defensive measure the investor might decide to hold off from the last roll. This would give the following horizon returns which would be very similar to the first roll-up strategy:

	$1.50	$1.55	$1.60	$1.65	$1.70
% yield	−15.75	−3.25	9.25	21.75	21.75

The same delta-adjusted strategy can be employed when the market falls and the strikes are rolled down:

Day 1: spot $1.60
Write $1.60 call (90 days) for 2.8 cents (delta 0.45).

Day 30: spot $1.56
Buy back $1.60 call (delta 0.25) for 1 cent
Write $1.55 (60 day) call (delta 0.5) for 2.7 cents.

Day 60: spot $1.51
Buy back $1.55 call (delta 0.24) for 1 cent.
Write $1.51 30 day call (delta 0.45) for 2.2 cents.

Day 90: horizon returns

	$1.40	$1.45	$1.50	$1.55 and above
% yield	−26.25	−13.75	−1.25	1.25

The results may not seem spectacular by any means but as a defensive action the strategy works effectively; the equity of the position is virtually preserved down to the $1.50 level which is a 10 cents fall from the original investment rate.

Rolling out: varying the maturity of the option

Writing shorter-dated options than for the precise maturity period and rolling out the position two or three times is an alternative method of increasing returns on any investment. The logic behind such a trading strategy is the fact that the premiums do not increase in a linear relationship with time; a three month option is not three times the premium of a one month option, for example, because the relationship between different option maturities and premiums is not time, but the square root of time. Thus in stable market conditions the option writer can gain more by writing three one month options in succession than from one three month call option. For example, using the same investment strategy as previously:

Day 1: spot $1.60
Write 45 day $1.60 call option for 2 cents.

Day 45: spot $1.60
Original 45 day $1.60 call option abandoned
Write second 45 day $1.60 call option for 2 cents.

Day 90: horizon returns

	$1.50	$1.55	$1.60	$1.65	$1.70
% yield	−5.5	9.5	19.5	19.5	19.5

Obviously, this very idealised example makes some rather unlikely assumptions about the movement in the spot market over a 45 day period (not to mention the underlying volatility of the option market) but it does illustrate how writing shorter-dated options can give better profitable opportunities. However, such a strategy demands much more active management of the option positions than with any of the previous examples because movement in the spot market over the life of the option will result in very different returns.

For example, assuming that instead of remaining unchanged the spot rate had fallen to $1.55 by day 45, the investor is faced with a difficult trading decision. His call option has expired worthless so that the premium of the original 45 day $1.60 call is his by right, but he now has to decide which option strike to sell – if any – for the second 45 days of the maturity period.

Writing a call option struck at the current spot rate of $1.55 will give a further premium income of 2 cents. Should the currency remain approximately at the $1.55 level for the next 45 days this will prove to have been the optimum strategy. But any rally in sterling back to the original spot level of $1.60 will reduce the overall return because the lower strike of the $1.55 call will limit the profit potential to this level.

Day 1: spot $1.60
Write 45 day $1.60 call for 2 cents.

Day 45: spot $1.55
$1.60 call expires worthless
Write 45 day $1.55 call for 2 cents.

Day 90: horizon returns

	$1.50	$1.55	$1.60	$1.65	$1.70
% yield	−5.5	7.0	7.0	7.0	7.0

Alternatively, should the investor believe that sterling will recover by the expiry date he could write another $1.60 call on day 45.

Day 1: spot $1.60
Write 45 day $1.60 call for 2 cents.

Day 45: spot $1.55
Write 45 day $1.60 call for 0.5 cents.

Day 90: horizon returns

	$1.50	$1.55	$1.60	$1.65	$1.70
% yield	−9.25	3.25	15.75	15.75	15.75

A similar rolling-out strategy could be adopted should the currency rally during the second 45 day period.

Day 1: spot $1.60
Write 45 day $1.60 call for 2 cents.

Day 45: spot $1.65
Buy back $1.60 call for 5 cents
Write 45 day $1.65 call for 2 cents.

Day 90: horizon returns

	$1.50	$1.55	$1.60	$1.65	$1.70
% yield	−18	−5.5	7.0	19.5	19.5

The rolling-out strategy can be employed defensively, by writing an in-the-money call option on day 45, or aggressively, by allowing the position extra profit potential by writing an out-of-the-money option.

Day 1: spot $1.60
Write 45 day $1.60 call for 2 cents.

Day 45: spot $1.60
Defensive strategy A:
Write 45 day $1.5750 call for 3.4 cents.
Aggressive strategy B:
Write 45 day $1.6250 call for 1.1 cents.

Day 90: horizon returns

	$1.50	$1.55	$1.60	$1.65	$1.70
% yield					
(A)	−2	10.5	16.75	16.75	16.75
(B)	−7.8	4.75	17.25	23.5	23.5

In conclusion, it can be seen that the decision to manage the option hedge, rather than to leave the short call option position 'lying idle' against the investment, is a trading one. Rolling up or down with the market is unlikely to work very successfully if pursued as a purely mechanical process, but like any trading decision should be undertaken with 'eyes wide open'. Of course this is no more than an extension of the original decision to hedge using currency options. In previous sections we discussed the selection of strikes as a reflection of market view, selling in-the-money call options as a defensive measure, writing out-of-the-money strikes in order to allow the position more profit opportunity in a rising market. Similarly each roll should be made on the basis of how the market is likely to perform and therefore what is the optimum strike or maturity to be selling.

The decision-making process is complex. It requires a more detailed knowledge of the option market than would be necessary for the simple buy/write strategy, and adequate option valuation software capable of providing suitable 'what if' analysis is also more than useful. Unfortunately, option pricing is not an exact science; although we know with certainty what the option premium will be worth on expiry given various levels in the underlying spot market, calculation of premium on an intermediate basis is a grey area, depending on such factors as implied volatility and interest rate differentials, and even on such intangibles as supply and demand in the option market itself and the bid/ask spread. Therefore, the whole process of evaluating complex strategies on an intermediate basis is vague and imprecise (probably for this reason most textbooks tend only to deal with rigid certainties of option values at expiration). Of course there is no obligation on the part of the option writer to manage his hedge actively; but for those investors wishing to use the strategies available in the currency options market to maximise potential returns it is probably necessary to know as much about options as the underlying investment itself, be it a deposit, a money market instrument, a stock, a commodity, or a bond.

Currency option trading strategies

The following analysis is by no means a comprehensive survey of all the strategy variations open to the option trader – concentration has been on the major themes, on the general rather than the specific. Some of the many publications which analyse in detail the variety of trading techniques available are listed in the bibliography.

Also, while some option strategies are universal to any market, stocks, bonds, commodities, etc., the final chapter in Part Three has been devoted to currency option trading techniques in particular. The nature of the foreign exchange market has meant that this concentration has been on exploiting and profiting from the effects of interest rate differential changes on currency option premiums.

However, before even attempting to describe any of the more esoteric option combinations it is important to explain why the straightforward option buying strategy is so attractive from a stock trader's point of view, but less so in the currency options market (where, by comparison, complex trading strategies have found a more appreciative audience). This factor is discussed in Chapter 9.

Why trade currency options?

Options or spot?

Compared to investing in equities, the business of option trading has always seemed highly dangerous and speculative, capable of producing spectacular profits but with the risk of total loss of the premium paid. The key to the success of the market has been the enormous leverage opportunities available. For example, see Figs 9.1, 9.2 and 9.3.

In percentage terms, the buyer of 100 ABC shares would show a return of 20 per cent (non-annualised) should the price rally from $100 to $120 within a month; the owner of the $100 call option, meanwhile, would show a profit of nearly six times his initial investment (566 per cent); the holder of the out-of-the-money $105 call would achieve a stellar 15-fold return. Moreover, given a sell-off in the market, the holder of the stock is risking a substantial dollar loss on any setback, whereas the option buyer can only lose the premium he originally paid away. The owner of the option has unlimited potential gains, and a limited loss; the owner of the stock also has unlimited potential gains, but his losses are also virtually unlimited (only limited by the fact that the stock cannot trade below zero). Hence the possibility of making extravagant gains while at the same time incurring a maximum and predetermined risk has attracted thousands of speculators to the stock options markets and has swelled the volumes on the options contracts on the Chicago Board Options Exchange (CBOE) to the point where the Exchange is the largest in the world, for options or futures.

The leverage associated with option buying is most spectacular when expressed in percentage terms; in absolute terms, however, the greater dollar profit is made from buying stocks, not options. The leverage effect remains, of course, but with the greater probability being that the stock price in one month's time will be trading closer to $100 than either $120 or $80 the stock owner will have at least maintained his equity (and may have some rights to a dividend); the option buyer, however, will have lost most, if not all, of his premium.

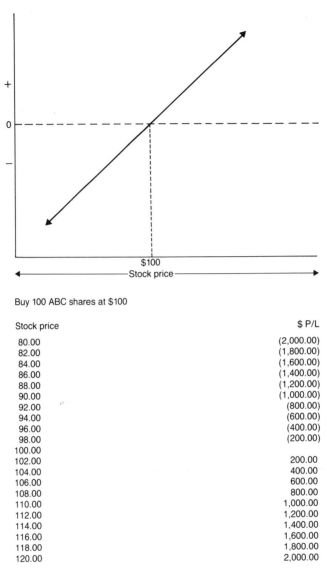

Buy 100 ABC shares at $100

Stock price	$ P/L
80.00	(2,000.00)
82.00	(1,800.00)
84.00	(1,600.00)
86.00	(1,400.00)
88.00	(1,200.00)
90.00	(1,000.00)
92.00	(800.00)
94.00	(600.00)
96.00	(400.00)
98.00	(200.00)
100.00	
102.00	200.00
104.00	400.00
106.00	600.00
108.00	800.00
110.00	1,000.00
112.00	1,200.00
114.00	1,400.00
116.00	1,600.00
118.00	1,800.00
120.00	2,000.00

Fig. 9.1   Buy stock.

In any case the concept of leverage in percentage terms is a dangerous and unreliable measure of performance as far as options are concerned. Out-of-the-money options are cheaper than at-, or in-the-money options; far out-of-the-money options cost very little in dollars and cents. But the chances of far out-of-the-money options ever becoming in-the-money are slim, to say the least. And even on the rare occasion that far out-of-the-

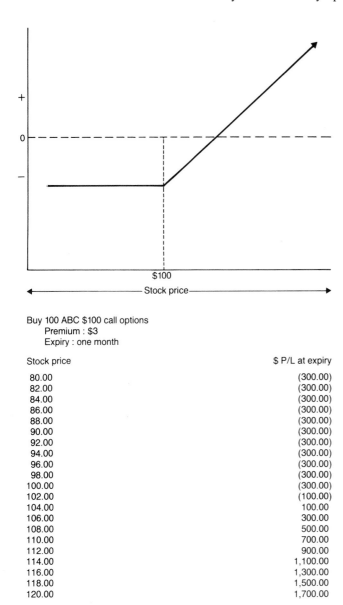

Buy 100 ABC $100 call options
    Premium : $3
    Expiry : one month

Stock price	$ P/L at expiry
80.00	(300.00)
82.00	(300.00)
84.00	(300.00)
86.00	(300.00)
88.00	(300.00)
90.00	(300.00)
92.00	(300.00)
94.00	(300.00)
96.00	(300.00)
98.00	(300.00)
100.00	(300.00)
102.00	(100.00)
104.00	100.00
106.00	300.00
108.00	500.00
110.00	700.00
112.00	900.00
114.00	1,100.00
116.00	1,300.00
118.00	1,500.00
120.00	1,700.00

Fig. 9.2   Buy stock options.

money option purchases prove profitable, claims made of several hundred per cent returns, while perhaps genuine, are not necessarily valid because the absolute profit is often very small.

Whereas in the stock market, gains of this magnitude are possible in a

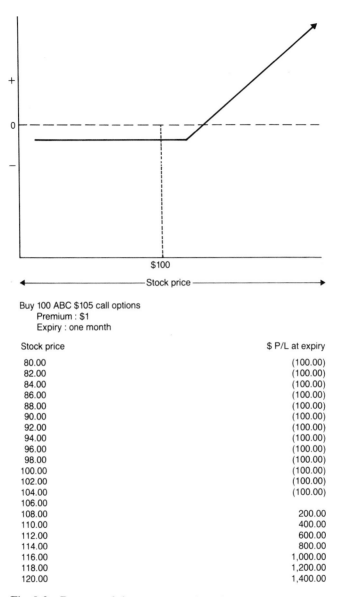

Buy 100 ABC $105 call options
  Premium : $1
  Expiry : one month

Stock price	$ P/L at expiry
80.00	(100.00)
82.00	(100.00)
84.00	(100.00)
86.00	(100.00)
88.00	(100.00)
90.00	(100.00)
92.00	(100.00)
94.00	(100.00)
96.00	(100.00)
98.00	(100.00)
100.00	(100.00)
102.00	(100.00)
104.00	(100.00)
106.00	
108.00	200.00
110.00	400.00
112.00	600.00
114.00	800.00
116.00	1,000.00
118.00	1,200.00
120.00	1,400.00

Fig. 9.3   Buy out-of-the-money stock options.

short space of time (for example during a take-over situation), such movements are far less likely in the foreign exchange markets where devaluations or revaluations of 20 per cent in a year are considered dramatic. Of course, with lower volatility in the currency markets, the premiums should be cheaper than for stock options, but the compensation is rarely sufficient to make the dollar profit on out-of-the-money currency options very attractive. The main reason for this, and the fact that the concept of percentage gain on an investment is even less valid with options on foreign exchange than for stock options, is because the cost of buying the underlying currency is essentially 'free'.

In the futures markets, for example, the cost of buying or selling is met by a margin payment; the amount varies according to the relevant exchange and by the currency (and the broker concerned) but it is normally a small percentage of the underlying contract value. This initial margin payment can be met by depositing interest-bearing collateral such as Treasury bills, or through the use of an irrevocable letter of credit issued in favour of the customer by another bank. The 'cost' of trading currency futures, therefore, is simply the cost of obtaining the letter of credit or the interest rate sacrificed between the Treasury bill rate (which the customer will receive) and the deposit rate in the market (which he would normally receive). This represents the real cost of trading currency futures, therefore (and also explains the enormous success of stock index futures markets where trading is possible for very large size, for low commissions, and for very low up-front funds).

In the foreign exchange market, for most banks and large financial institutions, the constraints on trading are not those of available funds but of market tolerance; a bank can only trade within the limits set by its own and other institutions, by its credit officers, and by the regulatory bodies such as the Bank of England. The costs of trading, as such, are effectively nil. For banks, large corporations and fund managers, the price of trading foreign exchange is the use of available lines of credit. Once these lines are used up, and the institution is unable to extend them or open new lines, it can no longer trade in the markets. For the better capitalised institutions, however, such lines are very large; it is possible, although of course not necessarily normal, for some institutions to take intra-day foreign exchange positions of several hundred million, and potentially billions of dollars.

The effect of this is that futures and foreign exchange trading are the most highly leveraged vehicles; any bank or investment manager who has a strong conviction in the markets can back his judgement in a very aggressive fashion. He has access to almost unlimited leverage. Even the private individual, assuming he can afford the initial margin payment, has enormous gearing opportunities. The margin cost is usually 2.5 to 3 per cent of the underlying contract value; this means that a move up or down of 2.5 to 3 per cent in the futures price will either double the initial 'investment' or eliminate it altogether. Trading futures is a two-edged sword.

It is possible to make speculative gains and losses. Using the same analogy as that given on page 2, a speculator who 'bets the house' on the futures market may make a 'killing' or he may find himself owing several times more than his original 'stake'.

Currency options buying, whether options on futures or on the physical currency, has the same risk/reward characteristics as buying options on equities. The opportunity to make spectacular gains still exists, but the maximum loss is limited to the premium paid. The trade-off is that currency options buying will never give the same absolute returns as spot trading.[1]

For example, Fig. 9.5 and Fig. 9.6 show the relative performance of buying a two week Deutschmark DM 2.00 put (at-the-money) and an out-of-the-money DM 2.05 put, both for amounts of DM 10 million, compared with the simple strategy of selling 10 million Deutschmarks at $/DM 2.00 in the spot or forward market (see Fig. 9.4).

The leverage of the spot-futures position results in larger profits and greater losses (both in absolute and in percentage terms) than with the option. Furthermore, not only is the performance of the option inferior to that of the spot or futures position on any rally, in a stable market the premium will fall in value whereas the spot or futures position is unchanged. In the real market, indeed, this effect is magnified because of the wider bid/ask spread in the option market and due to the risk in the option position of loss because of time decay (theta) and falling volatility (vega). Only with a sharp downturn in the market will the leverage of the spot/futures position work against the spot/futures trader and in favour of the option buyer.

An important conclusion can be drawn here; with equities, the leverage inherent in option buying can lead to large profits with the risk of losing all the premium paid. In the foreign exchange market the highest leverage (and the greatest profits) can be obtained by trading spot or futures. The spot/futures position can also result in substantial and potentially unlimited losses, whereas the maximum loss on any currency option purchased is the up-front premium paid. In the equity markets option trading is usually regarded as highly speculative and dangerous because the risks of losing the total investment, the premium, are high; by comparison, although the stock market can go down as well as up, the risks of losing the total investment in the comparable stock are low. In the foreign exchange markets the greatest risks and returns are in the spot market itself. Currency options are a conservative alternative providing lower risk, albeit coupled with lower returns.

---

[1] In special circumstances it is possible to make more from options than from spot or futures trading; see page 135 for some examples.

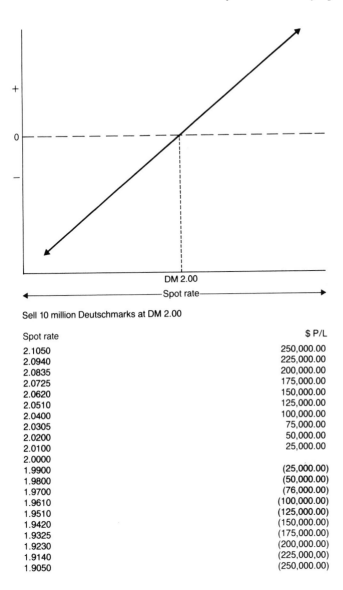

Sell 10 million Deutschmarks at DM 2.00

Spot rate	$ P/L
2.1050	250,000.00
2.0940	225,000.00
2.0835	200,000.00
2.0725	175,000.00
2.0620	150,000.00
2.0510	125,000.00
2.0400	100,000.00
2.0305	75,000.00
2.0200	50,000.00
2.0100	25,000.00
2.0000	
1.9900	(25,000.00)
1.9800	(50,000.00)
1.9700	(76,000.00)
1.9610	(100,000.00)
1.9510	(125,000.00)
1.9420	(150,000.00)
1.9325	(175,000.00)
1.9230	(200,000.00)
1.9140	(225,000,00)
1.9050	(250,000.00)

Fig. 9.4   Buy spot: Deutschmarks.

The main implication is this: anyone wishing to take a major position in any currency should trade the spot, not the option market; there is no substitute for holding the currency itself.

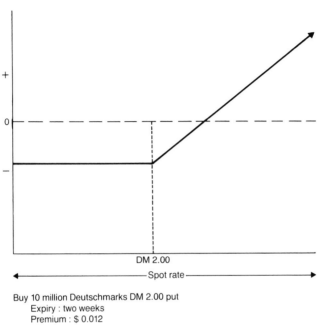

Buy 10 million Deutschmarks DM 2.00 put
   Expiry : two weeks
   Premium : $ 0.012

Spot rate	$ P/L at expiry
2.1050	130,000.00
2.0940	105,000.00
2.0835	80,000.00
2.0725	55,000.00
2.0610	30,000.00
2.0500	5,000.00
2.0400	(20,000.00)
2.0305	(45,000.00)
2.0200	(70,000.00)
2.0100	(95,000.00)
2.0000	(120,000.00)
1.9900	(120,000.00)
1.9800	(120,000.00)
1.9700	(120,000.00)
1.9600	(120,000.00)
1.9500	(120,000.00)
1.9400	(120,000.00)
1.9320	(120,000.00)
1.9230	(120,000.00)
1.9140	(120,000.00)
1.9040	(120,000.00)

Fig. 9.5   Buy at-the-money option: Deutschmarks.

Buy 10 million Deutschmarks two week DM 2.05 put
   Premium : $0.0065
   Expiry : two weeks

Spot rate	$ P/L at expiry
2.1050	63,000.00
2.0940	37,500.00
2.0835	13,000.00
2.0725	(12,000.00)
2.0620	(39,000.00)
2.0510	(65,000.00)
2.0410	(65,000.00)
2.0305	(65,000.00)
2.0200	(65,000.00)
2.0100	(65,000.00)
2.0000	(65,000.00)
1.9900	(65,000.00)
1.9800	(65,000.00)
1.9700	(65,000.00)
1.9600	(65,000.00)
1.9510	(65,000.00)
1.9420	(65,000.00)
1.9320	(65,000.00)
1.9230	(65,000.00)
1.9140	(65,000.00)
1.9050	(65,000.00)

Fig. 9.6   Buy out-of-the-money option: Deutschmarks.

Leverage in currency options

In highly volatile conditions when intra-day moves in the spot market are in the range of 1 per cent or more, a currency position of $10 million is liable to show a profit or loss of over $100,000; a trader unwilling to take such a risk is well-advised to limit his exposure substantially. Any such position run overnight carries even larger risks, of course. An option, however, gives the dealer the opportunity to trade much larger positions than he would normally take in the spot market, for substantially lower risk, and for much longer periods, days, weeks, or months.

This is the meaning of leverage in currency option markets. Options are highly leveraged instruments not because they are more profitable than spot trading – they are not – but because they allow the trader to take much larger than normal positions and for a longer time scale. An option to buy $100 million of Deutschmark puts might cost 2 per cent or $2 million, but the net profit should the dollar move up by 10 per cent within the maturity period of the option will be at least $7 million. A long spot position of $20 million would only show a profit of $2 million on such a rally but would incur an equivalent $2 million loss on a 10 per cent fall in the currency. Of course even a stable market would result in the total loss of the premium by expiration day. But the $20 million spot position would theoretically have a greater loss potential without the equivalent opportunity for profit.

A. Buy $100 million DM 2.00 put (US $ call) for 2 per cent ($2 million)
B. Buy $20 million spot/futures at DM 2.00.

	Profit or (loss) Spot $/DM	
	DM 1.80	DM 2.20
Spot trade	($2.2 MM)	$1.8 MM
Option trade	($2.0 MM)	$7.1 MM

Alternatively, the spot trader who is very bullish on the dollar might buy $100 million in Deutschmarks and risk losing $2 million – equivalent of about a 2 per cent fall in the dollar. The option trader could spend $2 million and buy $100 million of Deutschmark puts ($ calls). The potential loss is the same; the difference is that the option loss is up-front whereas the loss on the spot position is only estimated (in reality the risks inherent in any major sell-off are so enormous that few traders would have the authority, or would be willing to take the risks, of trading such amounts and particularly on an overnight basis).

On the other hand, the trader might buy options to the amount of the stop-loss he would usually put on his spot position; instead of buying $10 million at DM 1.80 and risking a 1 pfennig fall (equivalent to about a $30,000 loss) he might spend about $30,000 on Deutschmark at-the-money put options and thus establish a worst-case position in advance (see Fig. 9.7). He would have to buy quite short-dated options, however,

Buy 10 million Deutschmarks DM 1.80 put
   Expiry : one week
   Premium : $0.003

Spot rate	$ P/L at expiry
1.9058	278,000
1.8947	248,000.00
1.8837	217,000.00
1.8728	186,000.00
1.8620	155,000.00
1.8514	124,000.00
1.8409	93,000.00
1.8305	62,500.00
1.8202	32,000.00
1.8100	700.00
1.8000	(30,000.00)
1.7900	(30,000.00)
1.7800	(30,000.00)
1.7704	(30,000.00)
1.7600	(30,000.00)
1.7513	(30,000.00)
1.7419	(30,000.00)
1.7320	(30,000.00)
1.7234	(30,000.00)
1.7142	(30,000.00)
1.7052	(30,000.00)

Fig. 9.7   Buy call: Deutschmarks.

for the premium to cost the equivalent of only 1 pfennig. Alternatively, he might trade a synthetic put, selling Deutschmarks spot (buying dollars) and buying a Deutschmark call for about $30,000.[2] The call acts exactly like a stop-loss order (see Fig. 9.8). (There should be no difference – on expiry – in the performance of a put and a synthetic put except that the trader might prefer the greater control and liquidity inherent in owning the underlying spot position; also the wider spreads in the option market as well as the volatility risks may make it advantageous for the trader to buy spot currency and use the option as an insurance policy.)

How to outperform the spot market using currency options

One method of maximising potential gains using options rather than the underlying spot market is to use the concept of the delta and the gamma. The fact that the option premium will not increase or decrease in a linear fashion, that the hedge ratio (delta) changes as the underlying market changes, can be turned – in special circumstances – to the options' advantage. The diagrams on pages 137 and 138 compare the performance of a spot position (short DM 10 million) with that of an equivalent option position adjusted by the delta. Thus if at-the-money options have deltas of 0.5 it is possible to create an equivalent spot position by buying twice as many at-the-money options (see Fig. 9.9); similarly, buying three times as many options (with deltas of 0.33) as the underlying spot position replicates a spot transaction (see Fig. 9.10). On any immediate move the option trade will outperform the spot trade in both directions (see Fig. 9.11). This capitalises on what is known as premium convexity, the tendency for the premium value to accelerate or decelerate as the market moves up or down. As the underlying market moves higher, the two at-the-money options will increase in value faster than the spot position. If the market falls the options will lose value but less fast than the spot position. The further out-of-the-money the strikes, the more impact premium convexity will have on the profit or loss exposure of the option compared to the spot market exposure. Remember that both at- and out-of-the-money options are composed of time value only; time decay, particularly for very short-dated options, will eat very quickly into the profit potential of the strategy: for one week options even one day of stability in the markets will probably invalidate the option alternative (particularly if the implied volatility of the option market falls). But in the very short term the trade can be most effective. In special circumstances it is a rare example of a strategy with less risk and higher rewards.

---

[2] Discounting any effects due to interest rate differentials.

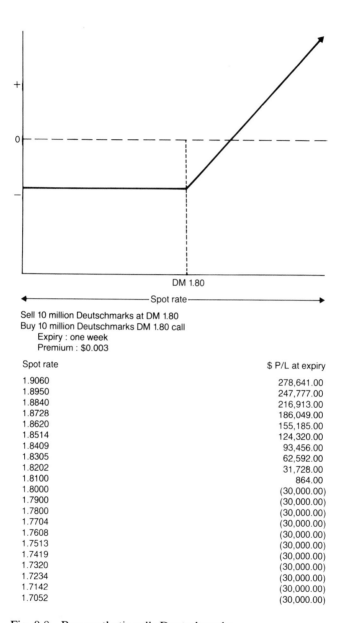

Sell 10 million Deutschmarks at DM 1.80
Buy 10 million Deutschmarks DM 1.80 call
    Expiry : one week
    Premium : $0.003

Spot rate	$ P/L at expiry
1.9060	278,641.00
1.8950	247,777.00
1.8840	216,913.00
1.8728	186,049.00
1.8620	155,185.00
1.8514	124,320.00
1.8409	93,456.00
1.8305	62,592.00
1.8202	31,728.00
1.8100	864.00
1.8000	(30,000.00)
1.7900	(30,000.00)
1.7800	(30,000.00)
1.7704	(30,000.00)
1.7608	(30,000.00)
1.7513	(30,000.00)
1.7419	(30,000.00)
1.7320	(30,000.00)
1.7234	(30,000.00)
1.7142	(30,000.00)
1.7052	(30,000.00)

Fig. 9.8   Buy synthetic call: Deutschmarks.

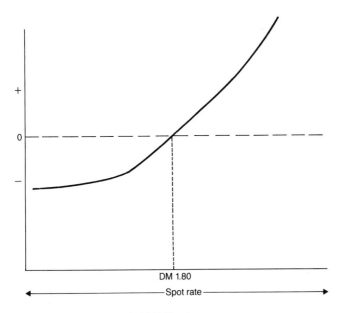

Buy 20 million Deutschmarks DM 1.80 put
    Delta : 0.5
    Expiry : one week
    Premium : $0.003

Spot rate	$ P/L on immediate move
1.8367	165,496
1.8329	145,174
1.8292	125,408
1.8255	106,308
1.8218	87,984
1.8181	70,547
1.8145	54,104
1.8108	38,749
1.8072	24,569
1.8036	11,633
1.8000	
1.7964	(10,440)
1.7928	(19,585)
1.7892	(27,500)
1.7857	(34,261)
1.7821	(39,956)
1.7786	(44,681)
1.7751	(48,542)
1.7716	(51,649)
1.7681	(54.107)
1.7647	(56,022)

Fig. 9.9   Delta-adjusted trade: Deutschmarks.

138   Currency option trading strategies

Buy 30 million Deutschmarks one week DM 1.81 put

Delta : 0.33
Expiry : one week
Premium : $0.0017

Spot rate	$ P/L on immediate move
1.8367	204,939
1.8329	177,116
1.8292	150,587
1.8255	125,513
1.8218	102,047
1.8181	80,321
1.8145	60,446
1.8108	42,517
1.8072	26,436
1.8036	12,278
1.8000	
1.7964	(10,510)
1.7928	(19,382)
1.7892	(26,760)
1.7857	(32,802)
1.7821	(37,672)
1.7786	(41,534)
1.7751	(44,547)
1.7716	(46,858)
1.7681	(48,601)
1.7647	(49,894)

Fig. 9.10   Delta-adjusted trade (2): Deutschmarks.

Sell 10 million Deutschmarks at DM 1.80

Spot rate	$ P/L
1.8370	112,000
1.8330	100,000
1.8290	88,000
1.8260	79,000
1.8220	67,000
1.8180	55,000
1.8145	44,000
1.8108	33,000
1.8072	22,000
1.8036	11,000
1.8000	
1.7964	(11,000)
1.7928	(22,000)
1.7894	(33,000)
1.7857	(44,500)
1.7823	(55,000)
1.7786	(67,000)
1.7754	(77,000)
1.7716	(89,000)
1.7681	(100,000)
1.7647	(111,000)

Fig. 9.11   Spot trade: Deutschmarks.

Some advantages of option trading

Therefore in answer to the question 'why trade currency options?' the market offers a leveraged trading opportunity with less risk (albeit normally, with less reward) than in the underlying spot or futures market. Indeed, because the risks involved in trading the spot market can be so high, most traders are forced to take very short-term positions. With option buying, however, where the loss is – so to speak – determined up-front by the premium paid, a trader can afford to run larger positions and for a longer period; he is secure in the knowledge that his maximum downside (the premium) has already been established.

For private investors or speculators, options give access to a market which may be effectively closed to them in any other form. For most private individuals and some small corporations there is no means of trading the spot or forward markets, or the transaction costs (spreads and commissions) are too great to allow for much short-term trading. Even in the futures markets, transaction costs can be high and the risks for smaller traders are significant; most reputable brokers advise their customers to trade futures only if the funds at risk comprise a low proportion of available risk capital. Options, however, are available to all. The costs of entering the market are simply the up-front premium. This is an advantage for small speculators willing to use a limited amount of risk capital as well as for some smaller corporate hedgers – particularly the one-man business which has foreign exchange exposure – for whom access through the options market is both simple and straightforward.

However, probably the main advantage in trading currency options is that an almost limitless variety of views can be mirrored through the many strategies available. A spot or futures trader can only buy or sell the currency. His trading opportunities are only two-dimensional. He can go long or short and he can adjust the size of his position to suit his views. But an option trader has many more trading opportunities open to him: he can trade direction, like a spot trader, and in some circumstances can create more highly leveraged positions (with less risk) than would be available in the spot market. He can take a view of the market stretching for days, weeks, months, or even years. He can take advantage of non-direction in the market and profit from stable as well as volatile conditions. He can trade interest rate differentials as effectively as any forward trader. To summarise, currency options offer the trader unique three-dimensional trading opportunities.

CHAPTER 10

Option trading strategies

Choosing the right strategy

As with futures trading it is a sad but true fact of life that the majority of option traders lose money. Many speculators make losses but continue to trade the markets in the hope that a sufficiently high percentage of trades will make money in order to offset the losing trades. In the stock market, for example, speculators will buy call options on stocks vulnerable to a take-over in anticipation of a high return should the market rumour prove justified. If the bid fails to materialise and the stock retreats, the premium will be lost but the exposure is less than if the trader had invested in the underlying stock itself. A series of small losses is tolerable if a genuine 'coup' occurs from time to time.

In the currency options markets some traders will deliberately accumulate far out-of-the-money calls and puts in stable conditions (when the premiums are likely to be low) in the hope of a major trend developing which will leave one or other of the options in-the-money before expiry. The chances are low that such a strategy will succeed, but the premium costs are also low and currency markets in particular do seem to have a tendency to 'trend' for longer periods than would be likely according to probability models. More often than not, however, traders lose money in the options market because of simple bad trading.

While there is no guaranteed method of making money in the currency options market – any more than in any other market – there are a few guidelines which, if followed, will save the option trader much unwarranted grief. These include the following:
1. There is no substitute for the correct view.

    Far from being a self-evident comment, if not a truism, there is a tendency for options traders, particularly those who are attracted to the market for the complexities of the strategies involved, to lose money or limit profitable opportunities due to an over-reliance on elaboration for its own sake. Similarly, to buy options because they appear 'cheap', to put together a strategy for 'something to do', or to construct a 'multi-dimensional' in preference to a simple transaction because of its inherent complexity rather than its potential profitability, are all recipes for disaster. It is vital before entering the market to decide on the view, and then to select the appropriate strategy to reflect that view.

2. Treat options as trading instruments in themselves, not substitutes for the underlying market.

    Of course, currency options are traded on the underlying currency and therefore move in relationship to the spot or forward markets, but this relationship is not constant; it depends on such factors as volatility, time decay, and premium convexity. Sometimes it is possible to buy a currency option and, because of time decay or volatility loss or other factors, to see the premium decline even when the underlying currency moves in the right direction. Usually, in such circumstances, it is preferable to liquidate the position immediately, incurring a small loss but saving further premium erosion. Even more so, if the market moves in the wrong direction it is usually best to cut the position rather than to wait and hope for an eventual turnaround. If the trader still believes that the original view was correct, rather than simply holding on to the option position he should look at other potential strategies for recouping profits on the trade. In other words, don't buy a three month option and leave the position lying idle in the hope that, in three months' time, 'something will turn up'; don't use option trading as an excuse for inactivity.

3. Use option strategies to trade options better.

    Far from the sceptics' view that complex strategies are a way for brokers to make more commission, some of the more elaborate

Market view: bullish

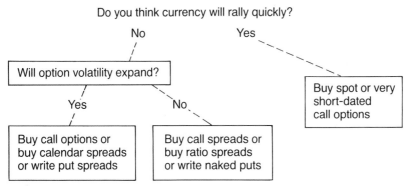

Fig. 10.1   Option trading decision tree (1).

Market view: bearish

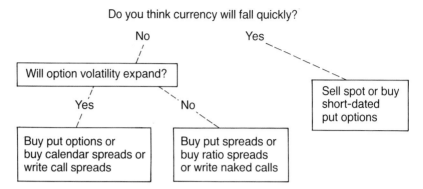

Fig. 10.2   Option trading decision tree (2).

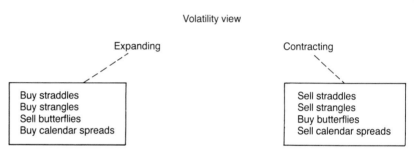

Fig. 10.3   Option trading decision tree (3).

trades are also very effective and profitable for the traders involved. As was mentioned previously, options are multi-dimensional products which offer opportunitites to the trader to profit from movements in volatility, interest rate differentials, direction, and time. Again, trading the more complex strategies for their own sake is definitely counter-productive; using the correct strategy to reflect a particular view is not just appropriate, it is what the currency options market is designed for. One method of analysing some of the various strategy alternatives available is through the use of a decision tree (see Figs 10.1, 10.2 and 10.3).

CHAPTER 11

The basic strategies

Buying short maturity options

As has already been demonstrated, with the exception of special circumstances the highest leverage can be obtained from buying the underlying spot or futures market. The buying of short-dated out-of-the-money call options is a close second to this strategy and has the advantage that, if the profit potential is less than with spot or futures, the exposure to the market if prices fall is substantially less. The major risk with such a strategy is that unless the anticipated move occurs almost immediately the loss of premium value through time decay (and probably through a fall in implied volatility) will make the chances of subsequent profits very slim.

The greatest leverage is obtained on options of less than a month's duration with strikes at- or slightly out-of-the-money (deltas of 0.5 to 0.3). Although leverage is high, such short maturity options have little or no flexibility; the trade is either right or wrong, wrong meaning no rally, not necessarily a falling market. A few days of stability in the underlying price and the premium is quickly lost. If the trade is successful the position can be liquidated or run, depending on the trader's view, but little follow-up action is necessary. If the market falls the option will lose value so quickly that this is one of the few occasions where there is little point in taking a loss as the premium recouped will be too low.

Buying very short-dated options can be a useful alternative to trading spot in situations where a contrary opinion of recent market direction is taken; for example, following a major sell-off when the market looks to be very over-sold, buying options is a safer alternative to buying the spot. If the trader is already short and wants to maintain his position he can give up some of his profits by buying 'insurance'. If the market continues to fall the underlying position is intact; if a technical rally does occur a 'stop-profit' is already in place. Also, in advance of an important economic or political event, such as an election, a trade figure release, or a key speech from a senior politician, a strategically placed short-dated option can capitalise on a sharp market move without jeopardising the trader's long-term view. Technical traders can position themselves with near-term options, buying calls or puts just above or below significant resistant or support levels. In all these cases the probability is that the premium will be lost but the insurance characteristics of the option outweigh the speculative risk/reward profile.

Buying medium to longer maturity options

Options should be purchased to capitalise on a strong and extended move in the currency, to buy 'time', to have the chance of making profits if the anticipated move takes several weeks rather than days, and to minimise risk. The selection of strike and maturity, as with most decisions in the option market, is a matter of a trade-off. Also the decision is different from the point of view of the trader from the hedger. Longer-dated options are worthwhile for the hedger because, in annualised terms, the premiums are much lower; for the trader the longer maturities have the disadvantage of offering less gearing. The highest leverage is obtained in very short-dated options, but the risks of time decay loss are also the highest. This is also the case with the selection of the strike. Far out-of-the-money options are 'cheap' and highly leveraged, but will only be profitable on a strong move in the market. In-the-money options sometimes appear attractive because the time value, and hence the exposure to time decay, is correspondingly less than for at- or out-of-the-money options, because the deltas are high, and therefore the premiums move faster into profit than for other strikes and because the break-even levels are lower (for call options) than for at or out-of-the-money options. Again, however, the greater premium cost for in-the-money options will result in lower percentage returns.

There is a contrast here between in-the-money equity and currency options. With equities, the purchase of in-the-money options can be compared to buying a partly-paid stock, with similar gearing opportunities. With currencies, however, an in-the-money option compares particularly poorly with buying the underlying spot or futures market; the higher premium cost means that the loss potential remains significant but the leverage is still much lower than with the currency itself. The premium has to be paid up-front, of course, whereas with the spot or futures position the maximum initial charge is at worst a small margin payment. Also, with futures the profits are received daily through the mark-to-market process but the profits on any option position are not received until the trade is closed out. With options on physical currencies, carrying a deep-in-the-money option rather than exercising into the underlying spot position can represent an opportunity loss. From a cash management view, therefore, the strategy of deep-in-the-money currency option purchases has little to recommend itself.

One possible strategy is to buy options with strikes slightly out-of-the-money (with deltas between 0.3 and 0.45). Further out-of-the-money options are too insensitive to spot movement and are too expensive to trade in terms of the lower liquidity and comparatively wide bid/ask spreads. Furthermore, as the market moves in the option's favour the deltas accelerate along the 'S' curve between the 0.3 and 0.4 level – the premium receives a 'kick' which is not evident in either in- or far out-of-the-money strikes.

Having selected a strike the decision remains as to the maturity of the option. A comparison of the risks and potential returns of different maturities can be seen in Table 11.1:

Table 11.1. Risks and returns: varying maturities.

Spot sterling $1.60	$1.62 call options		
	one month	three months	six months
Premium (cents)			
Day one	1.0	2.2	3.3
Day 21 spot $1.60	0.4	2.0	3.1
Day 21 spot $1.55	0	0.6	1.5
Day 21 spot $1.65	3.1	4.4	5.5

The decision as to which maturity to buy depends on the trader's view of the market. A strong and long-trending market would seem to favour the six month option, particularly if the move takes some time to develop. The longer maturity option is more expensive and, in percentage terms, performs the worst of the three maturities on a quick rally, but the position does at least buy time. Yet the losses on all three options given a 5 cent fall in sterling after three weeks are so substantial that none of the positions have much residual value; the six month option of course has the most premium remaining given such a move but the dollar loss is by far the greatest. There is a good deal to recommend the medium maturity, the three month option. The dollar cost is not too great, the time period of the option is more than sufficient for most trends to develop, and should the trader want to stay in the market as the price rallies there are several follow-up strategies which he can adopt.

Follow-up action for call option buyers

In a rising market

There are four actions which can be adopted as follow-up strategies once the market moves in the option buyer's favour:

Strategy A: Sell (take profits);
Strategy B: Do nothing (run position);
Strategy C: Roll-up;
Strategy D: Write higher strike call.

A and B need little further explanation. The decision whether or not to hold on to the position is the crux of any trading strategy, option-related or otherwise. Paradoxically, it is a decision about which there is little to say. The decision to buy an option is complex; it depends on the trader's view of the underlying market and the option market itself. But the decision to cut or run is based on more straightforward criteria. Is the rally going to continue? If so hold the position. Has the rally ended? If so liquidate. Running the position is the most aggressive strategy available; if successful, it will result in the greatest profits, but the risks are also highest. Selling the option is the most conservative of strategies, but is rarely the worst.

Strategy C, rolling up, is the process of selling the existing option position and buying a higher strike option; by doing this the trader hopes to maintain his profit potential while reducing his downside risk. The strategy is more conservative than simply holding the option but it has good profit-making opportunities nevertheless. It has the advantage of retaining the natural leverage of the option and can result, after two or three rolls, in a riskless position where a guaranteed profit is secured on any eventuality but the opportunity to make theoretically unlimited profits still remains. Essentially, once enough profit has been taken out of the original option to cover the purchase of the next higher strike, the trader is 'playing with someone else's money'.

There are two ways of rolling up. One, the normal method, is to sell the existing option when it has moved in-the-money by a reasonable amount, and to buy a higher strike. The second method, which is very aggressive but which can result in spectacular profits if successful, is to roll up the total premium received from selling the original option and invest the full amount in the next higher strike. This process is repeated until the trader decides to take profits. It is really an example of leverage on leverage. Table 11.2 shows an example of this.

The aggressive rolling up strategy works most impressively in idealised conditions, indeed it seems to be another example of using options to create higher profits with less risk (the alternative spot position, after all,

Table 11.2. Rolling up.

On 1 March, with spot sterling $1.60 and a three-month $1.64 call option premium 1.6 cents:

Day 1: spot $1.60.
Buy sterling one million 1 June $1.64 call for 1.6 cents or $16,000.

Day 10: spot $1.64. $1.64 1 June call: 3 cents.
                       $1.68 1 June call: 1.5 cents.
Sell sterling one million 1 June $1.64 call for 3 cents. (Receive $30,000.)
Buy sterling two million 1 June $1.68 call for 1.5 cents. (Pay $30,000.)

Day 20: spot $1.68. $1.68 1 June call: 3 cents.
                       $1.72 1 June call: 1.5 cents.
Sell sterling two million 1 June $1.68 call for 3 cents. (Receive $60,000.)
Buy sterling four million 1 June $1.72 call for 1.5 cents. (Pay $60,000.)

Day 30: spot $1.72. $1.72 1 June call: 2.7 cents.
                       $1.76 1 June call: 1.35 cents.
Sell sterling four million 1 June $1.72 call for 2.7 cents. (Receive $108,000.)
Buy sterling eight million 1 June $1.76 call for 1.35 cents. (Pay $108,000.)

Day 40: spot $1.76. $1.76 1 June call: 2.6 cents.
Sell sterling eight million 1 June $1.76 call for 2.6 cents.
Proceeds $208,000. Net profit = $208,000 − $16,000 = $192,000.
(Original 1 June $1.64 call worth 12 cents or $120,000 per sterling one million.
Net profit on 'buy and hold' $1.64 call = $120,000 − $16,000 = $104,000.
Profit on buy sterling one million spot at $1.60 = $160,000.)

---

makes only $160,000 with greater underlying risk). Of course the out-of-the-money options are always subject to time decay and volatility loss; they are composed of time value only and therefore are vulnerable to any subsequent set-back in the spot rate. But at no stage is the risk greater than the original $16,000 invested.

Strategy D, writing a higher strike call, is effective if the option holder feels that the main rally is over but there remains some limited upside potential. Selling a call against an existing position creates a bull call spread; the difference between this and the normal spread is that, by delaying the call write until the market has rallied, the trader hopes to receive at least as much premium from the option sale as was originally paid away to purchase the call. Consequently a locked-in profit is established whatever the subsequent market move.

An analysis of all four option follow-up strategies can be seen in Table 11.3.

It can be seen that there is no obvious 'best' strategy; it depends very much on the underlying market performance. Some obvious conclusions can be drawn, however:

1. Running the position.
    This is the most aggressive strategy, having the greatest potential profits and the greatest risks. There are two objections, however:

Table 11.3. Option follow-up strategies.

Day one (15 June): spot sterling $1.60.
Buy sterling one million 15 September $1.60 call for 3 cents.

Day 30: spot $1.65.   15 September $1.60 call: 5.6 cents.
                       15 September $1.65 call: 2.6 cents.

Net realised/unrealised profit or (loss)

1. Run position	$26,000
2. Sell position	$26,000
3. Sell $1.60 call/	
buy $1.65 call	0
4. Write $1.65 call	$52,000
(bull call spread)	

Day 60: spot $1.70.   15 September $1.60 call: 10 cents.
                       15 September $1.65 call: 5.2 cents.
                       15 September $1.70 call: 2 cents.

Net realised/unrealised profit or (loss)

1. Run position	$70,000
2. Liquidate position	$26,000
(Day 30)	
3. Sell $1.65 call/	$32,000
buy $1.70 call	
4. $1.60/$1.65 bull	$50,000
call spread	

Day 90:   Net profit or (loss) at expiry

	Spot sterling				
	$1.60	$1.65	$1.70	$1.75	$1.80
1. Run position	($30,000)	$20,000	$70,000	$120,000	$170,000
2. Cut position (Day 30)	$26,000	$26,000	$26,000	$26,000	$26,000
3. Roll-up (long $1.70 call)	$32,000	$32,000	$32,000	$82,000	$132,000
4. $1.60/$1.65 call spread	($4,000)	$46,000	$46,000	$46,000	$46,000

Firstly, it is inefficient not to attempt to maximise the return in an option trade; letting the position run is akin to leaving money lying 'idle on the table'. Secondly, once an option moves deep in-the-money it performs more and more like a spot position. In the above example the $1.60 call is worth little more than intrinsic value once the spot moves above the $1.66 level. In such circumstances the bullish trader is better advised to exercise or sell the option and buy the spot currency itself; the leverage is higher and the funds tied up in the position are less.

2.   Liquidating the position (taking profits).

Taking a profit is never a wrong decision, particularly if the trader feels that the spot market is about to undergo a correction. However, if the trader remains bullish a better strategy would be to roll up.

3. Rolling up.

    Rolling up the strikes in a bull market has two main advantages. First of all, it is a much better use of the trader's money than simply running a position (in the option market the old dictum 'run your profits' is not necessarily the best advice). Secondly, apart from a more efficient use of available funds, the strategy allows the trader the opportunity of benefiting from further rallies without risking his entire investment. Once the second roll has been executed it is usually 'free money' for the trader. The disadvantage is that, in perfect conditions, the profit potential is below that of the simple buy and hold strategy. However if the move is expected to be very strong the aggressive roll-up strategy, re-investing the entire premium on each roll, can of course outperform even the spot trade.

    Deciding when to roll and into which strike:

    As out-of-the-money options offer the highest leverage, the greatest profit potential is obtained from rolling from high into low delta strikes (although options with deltas below 0.25 are usually too insensitive to movement in the underlying currency unless a violent rally occurs). More conservatively, options could be sold when the delta moves into the 0.6 to 0.7 area, and new options bought with deltas of about 0.35. Too-frequent rolls and the transaction costs will erode the profitability of the trade. Also it is probably best not to continue to roll when the time to expiry is less than one month; better to roll 'out' into a longer maturity. At any stage, of course, should the trader feel that the rally has lost most of its momentum but that some upside potential remains, he can convert the long call into a bull call spread by writing a higher strike option against his existing position.

4. Writing a higher strike call.

    This is a conservative strategy but very effective if the higher strike can be written for a similar or greater premium than the original option purchase – in other words, if the trade can be put on for a small debit or even a net credit. The spread is particularly suitable in a gradually rising market, especially if implied volatility has also increased. Only a sharp decline would result in the erosion of all or most of the profit potential of the strategy.

In a declining market

A call option is purchased because the market is expected to move higher. When, instead, the currency falls, there are three main strategies which can be adopted. The first two are also the simplest.

Strategy A: Sell the option;
Strategy B: Run the position;
Strategy C: Roll down.

Strategy A is the simplest and very often the best strategy. Failure to take losses quickly (B) is usually the greatest failing of any option trader. The temptation is probably worse than for a spot trader because the option holder always has the fall-back that the premium, and therefore the loss, has already been taken; why, consequently, should he cut the position early? In fact, once the underlying currency moves in the wrong direction the chances of recouping any of the original premium paid diminish rapidly. The call is exposed to the ravages of time decay, and the possibility of volatility loss, and the premium will decline quickly and perhaps irretrievably unless some sort of remedial action is taken. The only occasion when running a losing position is the correct strategy is when the trader remains of the view that the currency will indeed rally.

Table 11.4. Rolling down and averaging down.

Day one: spot sterling $1.50
        Buy stg 1,000,000 90 day $1.50 call option for 3 cents

Day 30: spot sterling $1.47
        $1.50 call option 1.35 cents
        $1.46 call option 2.70 cents

Strategy alternatives
(A) Sell the option: loss = $16,500
(B) Run position: unrealised loss = $16,500
(C) Roll down:
sell stg 2,000,000 $1.50 calls for 1.35 cents (receive $27,000 premium)
buy stg 1,000,000 $1.46 call for 2.7 cents (cost $27,000)
Result of roll-down:
Long stg 1,000,000 $1.46 call/
short stg 1,000,000 $1.50 call. Net cost = 3 cents.
(D) Single roll down: sell stg 1,000,000 $1.50 call for 1.35 cents
                    buy stg 1,000,000 $1.46 call for 2.70 cents
    Net position: long stg 1,000,000 $1.46 call for 4.35 cents
(E) Average down: buy stg 1,000,000 $1.46 call for 2.7 cents
    Net position: long stg 2,000,000 $1.48 call for 2.85 cents
Profit or (loss) on expiry (day 90)

	Spot sterling			
	$1.40	$1.45	$1.50	$1.55
Strategy				
(A)	($16,500)	($16,500)	($16,500)	($16,500)
(B)	($30,000)	($30,000)	($30,000)	$20,000
(C)	($30,000)	($30,000)	$10,000	$10,000
(D)	($43,500)	($43,500)	($3,500)	$46,000
(E)	($57,000)	($57,000)	($17,000)	$83,000

Even here it may be preferable to cut losses early in order to reinstate the option trade at a later and more advantageous moment.

Rolling down as a defensive action (strategy C) involves selling twice the amount of existing call options and buying a lower strike call; the net effect is to convert the original long call option position into a 'money spread', in this case a 'bull call spread', with the short option strike at the same level as the original long option position.[1] Ideally the roll should be executed for no extra cost. The advantage of rolling down is that the break-even level on the original trade is lowered; the disadvantage is that the potential for upside gain is severely limited.

Other strategies, which are not normally to be recommended for defensive measures, but which are included for illustrative purposes, are the single roll down – selling the existing call and substituting a lower strike, and averaging down – buying lower strike calls to reduce the break-even level. For examples of these, see Table 11.4.

The main objection to these two strategies is that neither trade is defensive in nature. Faced with a situation where the market has turned against the option buyer, but where he still hopes to recoup some of the original premium, the roll down which converts a long call option into a bull call spread offers the best chances of return if the market moves back to the original spot level of $1.50. The break-even level on the trade is $1.49 ($1.46 + $0.03) which means that the trader has a reasonable opportunity of covering his costs. The simple roll-down and the average down strategies are purely aggressive; they would be attractive if the trader felt that rally was even more likely after the sell-off than before. Both are expensive trades, however; without a strong rally they will both turn out to be cases of 'throwing good money after bad'.

---

[1] See the next chapter for a fuller discussion of money spreads.

CHAPTER 12

Compound option strategies

Option strategies using writing as well as buying and writing techniques can be developed to trade a three-dimensional market view – of time, of interest rate differentials, of volatility, as well as simple direction.

Writing naked options

As an alternative to buying, option writing has the advantage that the premium cost is credited to the writer, not paid away. Therefore, in stable to rising markets (for put writers) or stable to lower prices (for call writers) the option seller is able to benefit completely from the premium income received. Also, when implied volatility is high, and expected to fall, the premium received from option writing can be attractive. This is the only real advantage, however. Not only is the premium received the only profit opportunity open to the writer however strong the market may move in the option's favour, but on any adverse move the loss can be substantial and certainly much greater than the original premium received.

For example, in Fig. 12.1 the option writer sells a three month SF 1.50 call option (US dollar put) on 10 million Swiss francs for $0.0175. The premium received, $175,000, is the maximum profit on the trade. On expiration, as long as the dollar is trading at SF 1.50 or higher, the premium remains with the option writer; any fall in the dollar, however, and the loss is theoretically almost unlimited. At SF 1.4150, for example, the loss is $225,000. Figure 12.2 illustrate the same strategy using sterling put options.

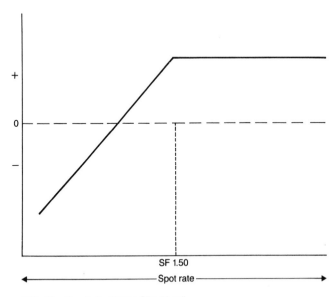

Write 10 million Swiss Francs SF 1.50 call

Expiry : three months
Premium : $0.0175

Spot rate	$ P/L at expiry
1.6070	175,000
1.5960	175,000
1.5845	175,000
1.5730	175,000
1.5600	175,000
1.5500	175,000
1.5400	175,000
1.5300	175,000
1.5200	175,000
1.5100	175,000
1.5000	175,000
1.4900	130,000
1.4802	86,000
1.4705	41,000
1.4610	(3,000)
1.4518	(46,000)
1.4421	(91,000)
1.4331	(136,000)
1.4240	(181,000)
1.4150	(225,000)
1.4060	(271,000)

Fig. 12.1   Naked write: Swiss francs.

Write 10 million sterling $1.60 put

Expiry : three months
Premium : $0.0425

Spot rate	$ P/L at expiry
1.5	(575,000.00)
1.51	(475,000.00)
1.52	(375,000.00)
1.53	(275,000.00)
1.54	(175,000.00)
1.55	(75,000.00)
1.56	25,000.00
1.57	125,000.00
1.58	225,000.00
1.59	325,000.00
1.6	425,000.00
1.61	425,000.00
1.62	425,000.00
1.63	425,000.00
1.64	425,000.00
1.65	425,000.00
1.66	425,000.00
1.67	425,000.00
1.68	425,000.00
1.69	425,000.00
1.7	425,000.00

Fig. 12.2   Naked write: sterling.

Spread trading

Debit money spreads

A money spread involves the buying of one option and the selling of another with the same maturity but with a different strike. Money spreads can be executed for a credit, when the option written has a higher premium than the option purchased, or vice versa, for a debit, when the option bought is more expensive than the option sold. In Fig. 12.3 a DM 2.00 put is bought for $0.012 and a DM 2.05 put written for $0.006. Both options expire on the same day (in three months). The net cost (debit) is the difference between the two premiums, or $60,000 per DM 10,000,000. Writing the DM 2.05 put creates two advantages over the simple put buying strategy; firstly, the premium cost is less ($60,000 against $120,000 for buying the DM 2.00 put). This also means that the break-even point on the position is closer to the spot than with the option buying strategy. The disadvantage of the trade is that the maximum potential profit is limited by the strike level of the written put option (DM 2.05). The maximum profit on any time spread can be calculated by subtracting the net debit on the spread – the up-front premium cost – from the difference between the two strikes. In this case the difference between the strikes is 5 pfennigs or approximately $122,000 per

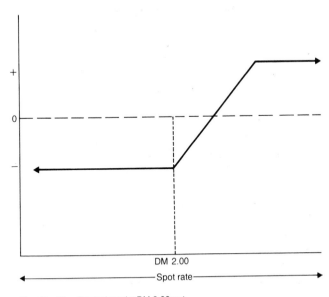

Buy 10 million Deutschmarks DM 2.00 put
    Premium : $0.012

Write 10 million Deutschmarks DM 2.05 put
    Premium : $0.006
    Expiry : three months

Spot rate	$ P/L at expiry
2.1000	61,950.00
2.0900	61,950.00
2.0800	61,950.00
2.0700	61,950.00
2.0600	61,950.00
2.0500	61,950.00
2.0408	40,000.00
2.0304	15,000.00
2.0202	(10,000.00)
2.0100	(35,000.00)
2.0000	(60,000.00)
1.9900	(60,000.00)
1.9800	(60,000.00)
1.9700	(60,000.00)
1.9600	(60,000.00)
1.9500	(60,000.00)
1.9410	(60,000.00)
1.9300	(60,000.00)
1.9200	(60,000.00)
1.9100	(60,000.00)
1.9000	(60,000.00)

Fig. 12.3   Money spread: Deutschmarks (at-the-money).

DM 10,000,000. Consequently the highest profit, when the US dollar is at DM 2.05 or above, is $122,000 − $60,000 = $62,000.

This may seem rather a poor risk/return profile but the spread is often an attractive, conservative trade to construct in 'normal' trading conditions. Most currency markets, after all, do not move by 10 or 20 per cent in three months; usually foreign exchange rates move much more slowly, or markets are characterised by sharp moves followed by substantial retracements. Money spreads are ideal vehicles in this environment.

The main disadvantage of such spreads is that on very dramatic moves in the spot market they tend to underperform the simple strategy of option buying substantially (see Fig. 12.4). Sometimes the spread will show an immediate loss even if the market moves in the right direction because the spread trade relies for its profitability on the time value premium decay of the written option position as well as the intrinsic value gain on the long option; if the move is immediate there is no time decay loss, indeed the short option position may even gain in value faster than the long position particularly, as is likely, if the move is accompanied by an increase in implied volatility. This inherent risk in spread trading is common to all option combination strategies. If the profit on the trade relies on 'squeezing out' the time premium from an option, any sharp move in spot is likely to show a loss, albeit temporarily, for the short option position.

As a corollary to this, however, money spreads work particularly effectively in periods when the spot moves gradually in the one direction and when implied volatility declines. In such an event, as the short option strike moves closer to the money, the effect of falling volatility will be greater than for the in-the-money long option which, by dint of its intrinsic value, is less subject to time decay loss.

Spreads can be constructed with in-, or out-of-the-money options. Ideally the optimum construction is for the lowest possible debit combined with the highest possible potential profit on expiry. As with simple option buying, the further out-of-the-money the two option strikes, the lower will be the net premium cost, and the greater will be the potential leverage of the trade; at the same time, however, the lower will be the probability that the trade will be successful (see Figs 12.5 and 12.6).

Credit money spreads

Whereas the naked short option position is a high risk/low return method of profiting from a moving market, a credit money spread is a low risk/low return alternative. A credit money spread is constructed by writing a naked option and then buying an out-of-the-money option as 'insurance' against an adverse market move. The spread is traded for a credit because

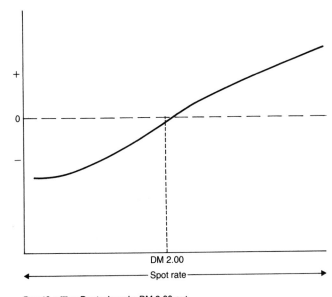

DM 2.00
◄———————— Spot rate ————————►

Buy 10 million Deutschmarks DM 2.00 put
   Premium : $0.006

Write 10 million Deutschmarks DM 2.05 put
   Premium : $0.012
   Expiry : three months

Spot rate	$ P/L on immediate move
2.0500	9,856.34
2.0460	8,492.24
2.0400	6,407.85
2.0350	4,226.13
2.0300	2,052.31
2.0250	(178.61)
2.0200	(2,382.16)
2.0150	(4,575.89)
2.0100	(6,759.41)
2.0050	(8,956.31)
2.0000	(11,159.71)
1.9950	(11,826.95)
1.9900	(12,093.69)
1.9850	(12,568.72)
1.9800	(14,314.22)
1.9750	(16,145.86)
1.9700	(18,016.97)
1.9650	(19,895.28)
1.9600	(21,789.57)
1.9550	(23,672.74)
1.9500	(25,543.25)

Fig. 12.4   Money spread (2): Deutschmarks.

Buy 10 million Deutschmarks three month DM 1.98 put
Premium : $0.015
Write 10 million Deutschmarks three month DM 2.03 put
Premium : $0.008
Expiry : three months

Spot rate	$ P/L at expiry
2.1000	54,400.00
2.0900	54,400.00
2.0800	54,400.00
2.0700	54,400.00
2.0600	54,400.00
2.0500	54,400.00
2.0400	54,400.00
2.0300	54,400.00
2.0200	30,000.00
2.0100	5,500.00
2.0000	(19,500.00)
1.9900	(44,500.00)
1.9801	(70,000.00)
1.9704	(70,000.00)
1.9600	(70,000.00)
1.9500	(70,000.00)
1.9400	(70,000.00)
1.9300	(70,000.00)
1.9200	(70,000.00)
1.9100	(70,000.00)
1.9000	(70,000.00)

Fig. 12.5   Money spread: Deutschmarks (in-the-money).

Buy 10 million Deutschmarks DM 2.02 put
Premium : $0.01

Write 10 million Deutschmarks DM 2.07 put
Premium : $0.005
Expiry : three months

Spot rate	$ P/L at expiry
2.1000	69,577.00
2.0900	69,577.00
2.0800	69,577.00
2.0700	69,577.00
2.0600	50,500.00
2.0500	25,500.00
2.0400	500.00
2.0300	(24,500.00)
2.0200	(50,000.00)
2.0100	(50,000.00)
2.0000	(50,000.00)
1.9900	(50,000.00)
1.9800	(50,000.00)
1.9700	(50,000.00)
1.9600	(50,000.00)
1.9500	(50,000.00)
1.9400	(50,000.00)
1.9300	(50,000.00)
1.9200	(50,000.00)
1.9100	(50,000.00)
1.9000	(50,000.00)

Fig. 12.6   Money spread: Deutschmarks (out-of-the-money).

the short option premium received is greater than the out-of-the-money premium paid away. Again, the maximum profit, at expiry, is the net premium received; the maximum loss is the difference between the strikes less the premium received.

For example, using the same naked short option as in Fig. 12.1, and adding a long SF 1.45 call option, converts the position into a credit spread (see Fig. 12.7). The maximum profit is $96,000, which is the credit received on the initiation of the trade; the maximum loss is $134,000, which is the difference between the strikes (SF 1.50 − SF 1.45) less the credit received.

Ratio spreads

The money spreads in the previous examples were all constructed on a one-to-one basis, for example buying a DM 2.00 put and writing a DM 2.05 put, both for DM 10,000,000. An alternative strategy, the ratio spread, is constructed by writing more options than are bought. The position can be traded on any ratio, such as buying one option and writing two (2:1) or three times as many (3:1) out-of-the-money options. The higher the ratio, the greater the risk and, correspondingly, the higher the potential return. The trade can be put on for a debit or a credit, although in the over-the-counter market it is often attractive to construct the spread for zero cost (see Figs 12.8 and 12.9). In such a way the position cannot lose money if the currency moves down (for a call ratio spread); on expiration day, the maximum profit is achieved if the spot rate is at the strike level of the short options positions (as with the simple money spread). Unlike the simple money spread, however, there is no maximum loss if the spot were to move substantially through the strike level. The trade can be profitable in any situation but is particularly worthwhile when implied volatility is high and expected to fall over the duration of the option (see Figs 12.10 and 12.11).

Butterfly spreads

Butterfly spreads are constructed by combining credit and debit money spreads. They are four-legged trades aimed at profiting from small but relatively precise currency market moves over the life of the option. The trade is put on for a debit, which is the maximum loss on the position. Maximum profit is achieved when the spot market moves to a particular level on expiration. In Fig. 12.12 an in-the-money ($1.55) sterling call option is purchased and an at-the-money $1.60 call written; this type of money spread is known as a bull call spread. Simultaneously, a $1.60 call is written and a $1.65 call purchased (a bear call spread). The two spreads

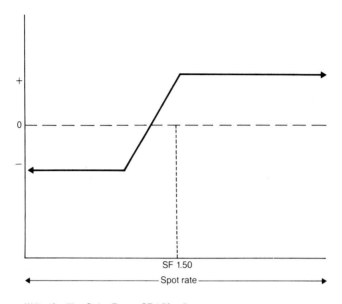

Write 10 million Swiss Francs SF 1.50 call
    Premium : $0.0175

Buy 10 million Swiss Francs SF 1.45 call
    Premium : $0.0079
    Expiry : three months

Spot rate	$ P/L at expiry
1.6000	96,000.00
1.5900	96,000.00
1.5800	96,000.00
1.5700	96,000.00
1.5600	96,000.00
1.5500	96,000.00
1.5400	96,000.00
1.5300	96,000.00
1.5200	96,000.00
1.5100	96,000.00
1.5000	96,000.00
1.4900	51,250.25
1.4802	7,000.00
1.4705	(38,000.00)
1.4610	(82,000.00)
1.4500	(134,000.00)
1.4400	(134,000.00)
1.4300	(134,000.00)
1.4200	(134,000.00)
1.4100	(134,000.00)
1.4000	(134,000.00)

Fig. 12.7   Credit money spread: Swiss francs.

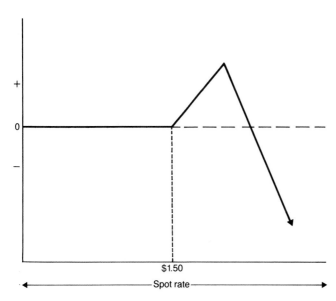

Buy £10 million sterling $1.50 call
    Premium : $0.0236

Write £20 million sterling $1.5350 call
    Premium : $0.0118
    Expiry : three months
    Volatility : 10 per cent

Spot rate	$ P/L at expiry
1.40	
1.41	
1.42	
1.43	
1.44	
1.45	
1.46	
1.47	
1.48	
1.49	
1.50	
1.51	100,000.00
1.52	200,000.00
1.53	300,000.00
1.54	300,000.00
1.55	200,000.00
1.56	100,000.00
1.57	
1.58	(100,000.00)
1.59	(200,000.00)
1.60	(300,000.00)

Fig. 12.8   Ratio spread: sterling (2:1).

Buy 10 million sterling $1.50 call
    Premium : $0.0255

Write 30 million sterling $1.5550 call
    Premium : $0.0085
    Expiry : three months
    Volatility : 10 per cent

Spot rate	$ P/L at expiry
1.40	
1.41	
1.42	
1.43	
1.44	
1.45	
1.46	
1.47	
1.48	
1.49	
1.50	
1.51	100,000.00
1.52	200,000.00
1.53	300,000.00
1.54	400,000.00
1.55	500,000.00
1.56	450,000.00
1.57	250,000.00
1.58	50,000.00
1.59	(150,000.00)
1.60	(350,000.00)

Fig. 12.9   Ratio spread: sterling (3:1).

Buy 10 million sterling $1.50 call
    Premium : $0.054

Write 20 million sterling $1.57 call
    Premium : $0.027
    Expiry : three months
    Volatility : 20 per cent

Spot rate	$ P/L at expiry
1.30	
1.32	
1.34	
1.36	
1.38	
1.40	
1.42	
1.44	
1.46	
1.48	
1.50	
1.52	200,000.00
1.54	400,000.00
1.56	600,000.00
1.58	600,000.00
1.60	400,000.00
1.62	200,000.00
1.64	
1.66	(200,000.00)
1.68	(400,000.00)
1.70	(600,000.00)

Fig. 12.10   Ratio spread: sterling (2:1).

Buy 10 million sterling $1.50 call
    Premium : $0.0525

Write 30 million sterling $1.62 call
    Premium : $0.0175
    Expiry : three months
    Volatility : 20 per cent

Spot rate	$ P/L at expiry
1.30	
1.32	
1.34	
1.36	
1.38	
1.40	
1.42	
1.44	
1.46	
1.48	
1.50	
1.52	200,000.00
1.54	400,000.00
1.56	600,000.00
1.58	800,000.00
1.60	1,000,000.00
1.62	1,200,000.00
1.64	800,000.00
1.66	400,000.00
1.68	
1.70	(400,000.00)

Fig. 12.11   Ratio spread: sterling (3:1).

together form the butterfly. The strategy achieves maximum profitability if the spot rate is precisely at $1.60 on expiry. The maximum loss is the initial debit ($120,000). The maximum profit can be calculated in butterfly spreads by subtracting the lowest strike ($1.55) from the written strike ($1.60) and deducting the up-front debit. Maximum loss is therefore $120,000 and maximum profit (with the spot rate at $1.60 on expiry) is $380,000. The risk/reward ratio consequently is 1:3 in this example. The ratio can be increased by using out-of-the-money options (Fig. 12.13 has a risk/reward ratio of 1:4). But as with any option buying strategy, from simple options to money spreads, the further out-of-the-money the strikes the lower is the premium and the higher the potential leverage – however, the probability of the trade being profitable is also correspondingly lower. Condor spreads are similar to butterflies except that the strikes are further apart. This gives the condor one advantage over the butterfly in that the maximum profit is attained if the spot rate trades within a predetermined range at expiration, rather than at a precise level. The trade-off is that the maximum profit potential (and therefore the risk/reward ratio) is substantially lower than for the butterfly spread (see Figs 12.14 and 12.15).

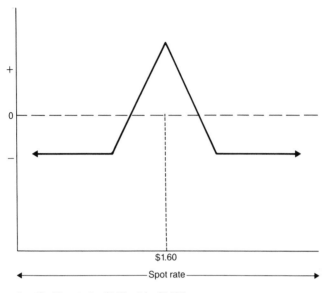

Buy 10 million sterling $1.55 call for $0.063

Write 20 million sterling $1.60 call for $0.034

Buy 10 million sterling $1.65 call for $0.017

Expiry : three months
Net debt : $120,000

Spot rate	$ P/L at expiry
1.50	(120,000.00)
1.51	(120,000.00)
1.52	(120,000.00)
1.53	(120,000.00)
1.54	(120,000.00)
1.55	(120,000.00)
1.56	(20,000.00)
1.57	80,000.00
1.58	180,000.00
1.59	280,000.00
1.60	380,000.00
1.61	280,000.00
1.62	180,000.00
1.63	80,000.00
1.64	(20,000.00)
1.65	(120,000.00)
1.66	(120,000.00)
1.67	(120,000.00)
1.68	(120,000.00)
1.69	(120,000.00)
1.70	(120,000.00)

Fig. 12.12   Butterfly spread: sterling.

Buy 10 million sterling $1.60 call for $0.035

Write 20 million sterling $1.65 call for $0.016

Buy 10 million sterling $1.70 call $0.0075

Expiry : three months
Net debt : $105,000

Spot rate	$ P/L at expiry
1.50	(105,000.00)
1.51	(105,000.00)
1.52	(105,000.00)
1.53	(105,000.00)
1.54	(105,000.00)
1.55	(105,000.00)
1.56	(105,000.00)
1.57	(105,000.00)
1.58	(105,000.00)
1.59	(105,000.00)
1.60	(105,000.00)
1.61	(5,000.00)
1.62	95,000.00
1.63	195,000.00
1.64	295,000.00
1.65	395,000.00
1.66	295,000.00
1.67	195,000.00
1.68	95,000.00
1.69	(5,000.00)
1.70	(105,000.00)

Fig. 12.13   Butterfly spread (2): sterling.

Trading volatility

Discussion of the volatility effects on various option strategies, such as money and ratio spreads, leads inevitably to an analysis of those strategies which are deliberately created in order to exploit changes in volatility. Volatility in this context is not simply the measure of dispersion, the standard deviation figure which is such a critical input in option pricing models. In reality implied volatility may decline in a gradually trending market; volatility, after all, is normally taken to mean deviation from a trend, not the trend itself. Some volatility trading is indeed directed at such changes in this implied measure, but normally, trades which are designed to make money in expanding or contracting volatility environments are essentially strategies built around a view of movement (or non-movement) in the market. The difference between the directional trade (option buying, money, ratio, and butterfly spreads) and the volatility trade, is that the directional trade is constructed to reflect a particular view of the direction of the market (prices moving higher or lower during a specific period); the volatility trade is designed to profit from a view of market activity. The directional trader needs to know if the

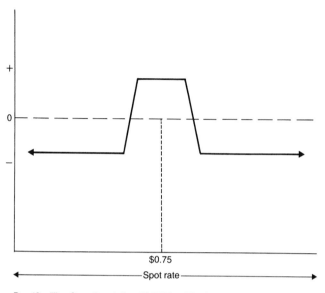

Buy 10 million Canadian dollars $0.7475 call for $0.0075

Write 10 million Canadian dollars $0.7500 call for $0.0062

Write 10 million Canadian dollars $0.7600 call for $0.0027

Buy 10 million Canadian dollars $0.7625 call for $0.0022

Expiry : threee months
Debits : $8,000

Spot rate	$ P/L at expiry
0.720	(8,000.00)
0.723	(8,000.00)
0.726	(8,000.00)
0.729	(8,000.00)
0.732	(8,000.00)
0.735	(8,000.00)
0.738	(8,000.00)
0.741	(8,000.00)
0.747	(8,000.00)
0.750	17,000.00
0.753	17,000.00
0.759	17,000.00
0.762	(3,000.00)
0.765	(8,000.00)
0.768	(8,000.00)
0.771	(8,000.00)
0.774	(8,000.00)
0.777	(8,000.00)
0.780	(8,000.00)

Fig. 12.14   Condor spread: Canadian dollars.

Buy 10 million Australian dollars 0.70 call for $0.009

Write 10 million Australian dollars 0.71 call for $0.0055

Write 10 million Australian dollars 0.72 call for $0.0033

Buy 10 million Australian dollars 0.73 call for $0.0018

Expiry : three months
Net debit : $20,000

Spot rate	$ P/L at expiry
0.648	(20,000.00)
0.652	(20,000.00)
0.656	(20,000.00)
0.660	(20,000.00)
0.664	(20,000.00)
0.668	(20,000.00)
0.672	(20,000.00)
0.676	(20,000.00)
0.680	(20,000.00)
0.684	(20,000.00)
0.688	(20,000.00)
0.692	(20,000.00)
0.696	(20,000.00)
0.700	(20,000.00)
0.704	20,000.00
0.708	60,000.00
0.712	80,000.00
0.716	80,000.00
0.720	80,000.00
0.724	40,000.00
0.728	
0.732	(20,000.00)
0.736	(20,000.00)
0.740	(20,000.00)
0.744	(20,000.00)
0.748	(20,000.00)
0.752	(20,000.00)

Fig. 12.15   Condor spread: Australian dollars.

market is going up or down (and perhaps in what time-scale). The volatility trader needs to know if the market is likely to trend, or not to trend, during a particular period; whether the market moves higher or lower is not as important to the volatility trader as whether the market moves at all.

Straddles and strangles

A long straddle, as in Fig. 12.16, is a position put on to benefit from large scale market movement in either direction. A call and a put option of the same strike and maturity are both purchased simultaneously; in our example, the strikes happen to be at-the-money although there is no hard and fast rule about this. The $1.50 call costs 3 cents and the $1.50 put costs

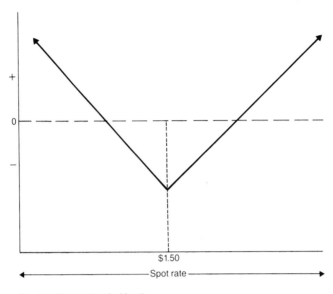

Buy 10 million sterling $1.50 call

    Premium : $0.03

Buy 10 million sterling $1.50 put

    Premium : $0.04
    Expiry : three months

Spot rate	$ P/L at expiry
1.30	1,300,000.00
1.32	1,100,000.00
1.34	900,000.00
1.36	700,000.00
1.38	500,000.00
1.40	300,000.00
1.42	100,000.00
1.44	(100,000.00)
1.46	(300,000.00)
1.48	(500,000.00)
1.50	(700,000.00)
1.52	(500,000.00)
1.54	(300,000.00)
1.56	(100,000.00)
1.58	100,000.00
1.60	300,000.00
1.62	500,000.00
1.64	700,000.00
1.66	900,000.00
1.68	1,100,000.00
1.70	1,300,000.00

Fig. 12.16   Long straddle: sterling.

4 cents; the total premium cost, therefore, is $700,000 per 10 million pound straddle position. At expiration, for the straddle to break even, sterling must be either 7 cents higher or lower than the strike; the break-even rate is therefore $1.57 or $1.43. Any major move outside this range has potentially unlimited opportunity for profit.

The long strangle (see Fig. 12.17) differs from the straddle in that the strikes are not the same; in our example the $1.54 call and $1.44 put option are both purchased for a combined cost of 3.1 cents or $310,000 per 10 million pounds. The cost of the strangle is lower than that of the straddle, but the break-even rate is further from the original spot rate; the break-even rates in our example are $1.4090 and $1.5710 (calculated by subtracting the initial premium cost from the put strike and adding it to the call strike). Also the strangle is less profitable than the straddle on an equivalent move.

By writing straddles or strangles (see Figs 12.18 and 12.19), the trader can profit in stagnant or reasonably stable conditions. Obviously the risks and rewards are inverted compared to the long positions; a short straddle or strangle has a maximum profit (the premium received) but is subject to potentially unlimited loss. In this sense it is very similar to the simple naked write strategy; the only difference is that the straddle or strangle has twice the risk (the trade can lose money in either direction) but twice the reward. But realistically, as long as the trader is disciplined, short volatility positions can be very profitable and can often be unwound shortly before expiry for virtually all the potential profit.

Implied volatility is naturally a significant factor in either buying or selling volatility. In periods of low implied volatility long straddles or strangles are more attractive than when options are comparatively more expensive (when writing options becomes more viable). Low volatility conditions also offer good opportunities for traders to put on backspreads.

Backspreads

The backspread is another strategy which aims to benefit from expanding volatility in either direction; it differs from the straddle or strangle in that it is more highly leveraged (in one direction) and can be traded on a very short- as well as long-term horizon. Backspreads can be put on entirely with options but my preference is to combine the spot and the option position. The usual construction is to buy the underlying currency and to buy put options on a delta basis (twice as many puts with 0.5 deltas, three times as many with 0.33 deltas etc.). The trade can be engineered in the opposite way using call options, in this case selling the currency and buying currency calls on a delta based ratio. The further out-of-the-

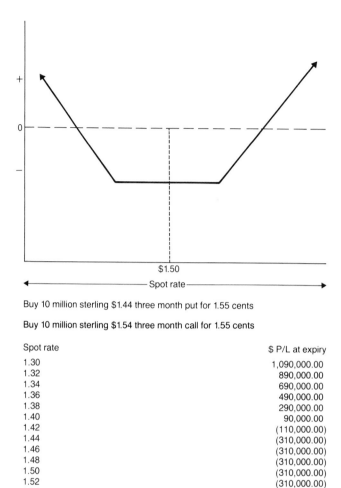

Buy 10 million sterling $1.44 three month put for 1.55 cents

Buy 10 million sterling $1.54 three month call for 1.55 cents

Spot rate	$ P/L at expiry
1.30	1,090,000.00
1.32	890,000.00
1.34	690,000.00
1.36	490,000.00
1.38	290,000.00
1.40	90,000.00
1.42	(110,000.00)
1.44	(310,000.00)
1.46	(310,000.00)
1.48	(310,000.00)
1.50	(310,000.00)
1.52	(310,000.00)
1.54	(310,000.00)
1.56	(110,000.00)
1.58	90,000.00
1.60	290,000.00
1.62	490,000.00
1.64	690,000.00
1.66	890,000.00
1.68	1,090,000.00
1.70	1,290,000.00

Fig. 12.17   Long strangle: sterling.

money the options (lower deltas), the greater the potential leverage in the backspread, but as with all out-of-the-money option positions, the higher the leverage the greater the probability that the trade will lose money. Backspreads are really no more than an extension of a synthetic position;

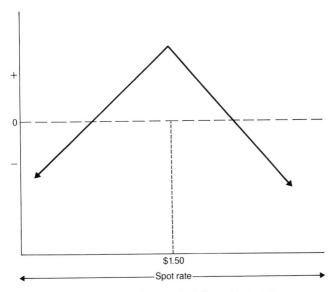

$1.50

←——————————— Spot rate ———————————→

Write 10 million sterling $1.50 three month sterling put for 4 cents

Write 10 million sterling $1.50 three month sterling call for 3 cents

Spot rate	$ P/L at expiry
1.30	(1,300,000.00)
1.32	(1,100,000.00)
1.34	(900,000.00)
1.36	(700,000.00)
1.38	(500,000.00)
1.40	(300,000.00)
1.42	(100,000.00)
1.44	100,000.00
1.46	300,000.00
1.48	500,000.00
1.50	700,000.00
1.52	500,000.00
1.54	300,000.00
1.56	100,000.00
1.58	(100,000.00)
1.60	(300,000.00)
1.62	(500,000.00)
1.64	(700,000.00)
1.66	(900,000.00)
1.68	(1,100,000.00)
1.70	(1,300,000.00)

Fig. 12.18   Short straddle: sterling.

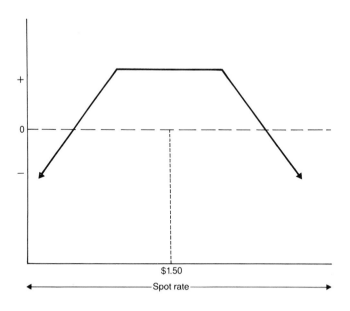

Write 10 million sterling $1.44 three month put for 1.55 cents

Write 10 million sterling $1.54 three month call for 1.55 cents

Spot rate	$ P/L at expiry
1.30	(1,090,000.00)
1.32	(890,000.00)
1.34	(690,000.00)
1.36	(490,000.00)
1.38	(290,000.00)
1.40	(90,000.00)
1.42	110,000.00
1.44	310,000.00
1.46	310,000.00
1.48	310,000.00
1.50	310,000.00
1.52	310,000.00
1.54	310,000.00
1.56	110,000.00
1.58	(90,000.00)
1.60	(290,000.00)
1.62	(490,000.00)
1.64	(690,000.00)
1.66	(890,000.00)
1.68	(1,090,000.00)
1.70	(1,290,000.00)

Fig. 12.19   Short strangle: sterling.

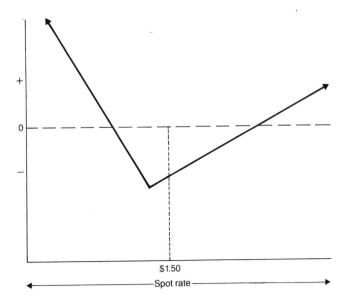

Buy 1 million sterling spot at $1.50

Buy 3 million sterling $1.4750 put for 1.1 cents

Expiry : one month
Premium : $0.011

Spot rate	$ P/L at expiry
1.38	132,000.00
1.39	112,000.00
1.40	92,000.00
1.41	72,000.00
1.42	52,000.00
1.43	32,000.00
1.44	12,000.00
1.45	(8,000.00)
1.46	(28,000.00)
1.47	(48,000.00)
1.48	(53,000.00)
1.49	(43,000.00)
1.50	(33,000.00)
1.51	(23,000.00)
1.52	(13,000.00)
1.53	(3,000.00)
1.54	7,000.00
1.55	17,000.00
1.56	27,000.00
1.57	37,000.00
1.58	47,000.00
1.59	57,000.00
1.60	67,000.00
1.61	77,000.00
1.62	87,000.00

Fig. 12.20   Backspread: sterling.

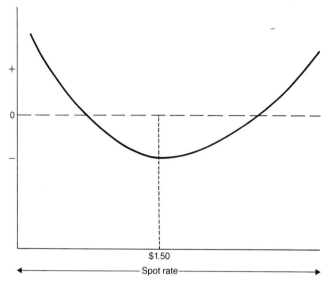

Buy 1 million sterling spot at $1.50

Buy 3 million sterling $1.4750 one month put for 1.1 cents

Spot rate	$ P/L on immediate move
1.450	19,688
1.455	14,651
1.460	10,184
1.465	6,310
1.470	3,047
1.475	410
1.480	(1,680)
1.485	(3,153)
1.490	(4,026)
1.495	(4,323)
1.500	(4,071)
1.505	(3,300)
1.510	(2,039)
1.515	(324)
1.520	1,811
1.525	4,331
1.530	7,200
1.535	10,382
1.540	13,843
1.545	17,550
1.550	21,471

Fig. 12.21   Backspread (2): sterling.

as buying the spot and buying a put option creates a synthetic long call position, or as selling the spot currency and buying a call option creates a synthetic put option, so backspreads are essentially a highly leveraged version of the same strategy. Of course, as with any leveraged option position, time decay and stable markets are anathema to the backspread strategy. The advantage is that not only on expiry will the trade make substantial profits on any major market move, but even on a short-term basis the leverage in the option position, otherwise known as premium convexity – the tendency for the premium to accelerate as the strike moves in the money – can provide good trading opportunities.

In Fig. 12.20, one million pounds spot is bought at $1.50 and three million pounds of one month $1.4750 puts (deltas 0.33) are bought for 1.1 cents ($33,000). The maximum loss on expiry is $58,000 at a spot rate of $1.4750; this represents the premium paid plus the foreign exchange loss ($1.50 – $1.4750 = 2.5 cents or $25,000 per stg one million). The trade is biased towards the downside on sterling because the three million pounds of put options represent a higher potential position than the existing £1 million long position. (On a strong rally the backspread converts into a long £1 million spot position and the puts will be abandoned; on any sell-off the long spot position is offset by one million pounds of the long put option leaving the trader the opportunity of exercising the two million pounds worth of puts remaining.) Therefore, if the trader has a particular view of the market he should construct his backspread accordingly. For example, if he feels that sterling is more likely to rally than decline he should sell the pound spot and buy call options using a delta ratio.

On an immediate basis (Fig. 12.21), the backspread will also make money as long as the market is moving. Here time decay is a serious issue, however; any large move of 3–4 cents will be profitable in either direction, and the whole trade can be liquidated on the same day if a reasonable profit is obtained even within an hour of opening the strategy. (Beware of the bid/ask spread in these circumstances, however.) But if the currency markets stabilise for any period the combination of falling implied volatility and time decay loss will quickly erode the profit potential in the strategy. If markets look as if they are beginning to consolidate, the best action may well be to close out the position rather than take a greater loss by expiry.

CHAPTER 13

Currency option trading techniques

Currency options and interest rate differentials

The factor which dictates the forward price of a currency, interest rate parity, also has a crucial role in determining the premium for a currency option. In Part One we saw that the reason why Deutschmark call options, for example, usually trade at a higher premium to Deutschmark puts, both at the same strike, is purely a function of interest rate parity; Deutschmarks trade at a premium forward because Deutschmark interest rates are lower than US dollar interest rates, and this forward premium must be reflected in the call option premium (although not in the put option). In theory the forward rate is the best guess price of a currency at a future date. In fact the forward is no such thing; the Swiss franc, for example, has consistently traded at a premium forward to the US dollar for 20 years or more, yet the dollar has had periods of great strength and weakness during this time. The forward price is simply the foreign exchange rate at which interest rate arbitrage achieves parity; and the level of interest rates is, among many other factors, dictated by the present or anticipated level of inflation in a country. But although there may be some long term correlation between a higher interest rate environment, higher inflation, and a weak currency (sterling, lira, Australian dollars, for example), and a lower interest rate environment, lower inflation, and a strong currency (Swiss francs, Deutschmarks, Japanese yen, for example), the link in the short to medium term is tenuous to say the least.

If this is the case, currency option strategies can be constructed to exploit this imperfect relationship. Apparent anomalies can sometimes occur in currency option pricing which can offer interesting trading opportunities. Usually, these 'anomalies' are to be found where interest rate differentials are large, such as with Australian or New Zealand dollars, or with cross-rates such as sterling against the Deutschmark. For example, at the end of January 1987 sterling, which had been under pressure in the foreign exchange markets alongside the US dollar, had fallen to a rate of DM 2.77 against the Deutschmark. Because of the effect of interest rate differentials (as well as a variation in implied volatility between different option maturities) the following spot, forward, and option relationships could be found:

23 January 1987
Sterling/Deutschmark spot: DM 2.77
Sterling interest rates (three months and 12 months) 11 per cent.
Deutschmark interest rates (three months and 12 months) 4 per cent.
Sterling/Deutschmark three months forward: DM 2.72
   Three months DM 2.77 sterling call/Deutschmark put,
   European style: 1.14 per cent or 3.15 pfennigs per pound.
Sterling/Deutschmark 12 months forward: DM 2.59
   12 months DM 2.77 sterling call/Deutschmark put,
   European style: 1.14 per cent or 3.15 pfennigs per pound.

The fact that a one year option was trading at the same premium as a three month option with the same strike is testimony, not to imperfections in the option market, but to the effects of the large interest rate differentials between sterling and Deutschmarks (and therefore the large discount for sterling 12 months forward), on the valuation of European options. Because European options cannot be exercised early, the only arbitrage opportunity is against the forward rate, not the spot. Consequently, the DM 2.77 12 months option, although struck at the spot rate, is in fact 7 per cent out-of-the-money versus the forward outright; the three months option, however, is only 1.8 per cent out-of-the-money versus the forward.

At first glance it might seem a riskless trade to sell the three month and buy the one year option. This would create a time, or calendar spread (a strategy which will be analysed in greater detail later in this chapter) for no cost. If the sterling/Deutschmark spot rate in three months' time is around the same DM 2.77 level (or indeed lower) the trader has in fact established a long sterling call/Deutschmark put, expiring in nine months, for free. Unfortunately, on any rally in sterling over the ensuing three months the premium for the short three month option will rise in value faster than the long 12 month option. This is simply because the delta of the short option (0.4) is higher than the delta of the long option (0.2); thus on any rally the premium of the former will increase in value faster than the premium of the latter. In fact, on the expiry of the three month option, at the end of April 1987, the following relationships applied:

Sterling/Deutschmark spot rate: DM 2.98
Loss on short DM 2.77 sterling call: 21 pfennigs or 7.05 per cent.

Value of 9 months DM 2.77 sterling call/Deutschmark put, European style:
14.3 pfennigs or 4.85 per cent.
Net loss on position: 6.7 pfennigs or 2.25 per cent.

In reality the loss on the strategy would have been greater had not sterling interest rates fallen to 9 per cent by this time and the interest rate differential narrowed to nearly 5 per cent. If the differential had remained at 7 per cent the value of the nine month option would have been even lower because the DM 2.77 call would still have been out-of-the-money versus the nine month forward rate. Thus if interest rate differentials had remained unchanged the DM 2.77 nine month option would only have been worth 12 pfennigs instead of 14.3, and the net loss (if the trade had been closed out at this point) would have been 9 pfennigs or 3.03 per cent.

Exploiting the effect of interest rate differentials

If the time spread strategy will not create riskless profits it does nevertheless point to a means of exploiting the interest rate differential effect on currency options. For example, take the different premiums for European and American style options; European calls on higher interest rate currencies (like sterling) or puts on lower interest rate currencies (like Deutschmarks) are always cheaper than their American equivalents. Therefore, for traders wishing to buy calls on higher interest currencies, or buy puts on lower interest rate currencies, European options have a lower premium and, consequently, offer higher leverage. Take Australian dollars, for example:

Day 1: (All underlying amounts $ Australian 1,000,000).
Strategy A: Buy 6 months $ Australian call at-the-money spot, American style, for 1.4 cents or $US 14,000
Strategy B: Buy 6 months $ Australian call at-the-money spot, European style, for 1.1 cents or $US 11,000

Profit or loss after three months:
Spot $ Australian (movement in US cents per $ Australian)

	−10	−5	−2.5	0	+2.5	+5	+10
A.	−$14,000	−$14,000	−$11,000	−$3,000	+$12,000	+$36,000	+$84,000
B.	−$11,000	−$11,000	−$9,000	−$1,000	+$12,000	+$27,000	+$70,000

Profit or loss on expiry:

	−10	−5	−2.5	0	+2.5	+5	+10
A.	−$14,000	−$14,000	−$14,000	−$14,000	+$11,000	+$36,000	+$84,000
B.	−$11,000	−$11,000	−$11,000	−$11,000	+$14,000	+$39,000	+$87,000

Although the absolute profit potential of the American style option is greater if the Australian dollar rallies quickly, the leverage of the

European option is nevertheless higher because the initial premium cost is less. If the rally is of longer duration the European option will give both higher absolute profits as well as substantially higher leverage.

The differences between the pricing of currency options can be exploited in other ways. For example, the foreign exchange market nowadays can be seen in terms of currency blocs rather than individual trading units. If the dollar is falling it is falling not only against the Deutschmark but also against the Italian lira, at least to the extent that the lira is linked to the Deutschmark inside the EMS mechanism. If the lira is devalued against the Deutschmark during this period then the decline in the $/lira may well be less than the equivalent move in the $/ Deutschmark. If the dollar fall is sufficiently extended there may be offsetting benefits in buying lira call options rather than Deutschmark call options, particularly when lira options are cheaper. If the lira is seen as too risky a currency to trade (perhaps because the EMS tolerances are wider than for other currencies) then options on the ECU may well be an attractive alternative to the buying of Deutschmark call options. Essentially, the strategy is worth exploring if the trader's view is on the US dollar itself rather than on a particular currency against the US dollar, and the extent of the anticipated move is great enough to compensate for smaller fluctuations within other currency relationships. For example;

2 September 1986
Spot ECU/$: $1.0353 per ECU
Strategy A: Buy 6 month at-the-money-spot ECU call, American style, for 3.70 per cent or $37,000 per $US 1,000,000

Spot $/Deutschmark: DM 2.02670 per $US
Strategy B: Buy 6 month at-the-money-spot DM call, American or European, for 4.6 per cent or $46,000 per $US 1,000,000

1 March 1987
Spot ECU: $1.1303
Spot $/DM: DM 1.8260

Net profit on option purchases:
Strategy 1 (ECU): $55,700
percentage return: 148%

Strategy 2 (DM): $63,500
percentage return: 138%

The rally in Deutschmarks was greater than for ECUs during this period (9.87 per cent against 9.17 per cent) but because the ECU call option premium cost substantially less than the Deutschmark option the returns on the ECU option were higher. Implied volatility for ECU and Deutschmark options were very similar on 2 September but the

Deutschmark call option was more expensive simply because the cost of the forward points was reflected in the premium, (because the Deutschmark forward was at a premium to the spot rate the at-the-money call struck at the spot rate was in-the-money versus the forward). ECU interest rates were higher than for US dollars and therefore the ECU was at a discount forward; thus the ECU call option, at-the-money spot, was out-of-the-money versus the forward, and consequently cheaper. In this particular case ECU rates were not sufficiently above those of US dollars to make the European option worth buying (the European call would have cost only $500 less than the American option). But in circumstances where interest rate differentials are large the saving in premium for the European option may be enough to offset the risk that the currency rallies so quickly that the European option underperforms the American equivalent.

Calendar (time) spreads

A time or calendar spread is a strategy which can take advantage of directional and volatility movement in the market, is designed to exploit the time decay effects of options with different maturities, and can also profit from movement in interest rate differentials. An extreme illustration of the trade has already been given using the sterling/Deutschmark option; but other more actively traded options markets respond well to such a strategy. For example, the trade outlined in Fig. 13.1 is constructed to conform to the following view:

1. The dollar/yen rate, currently Y 138.50, will move sideways over the next two months.
2. Implied volatility of the market (10 per cent) is too low by comparison with historical data, or according to the view of the trader. In spite of his view of the likely lack of market direction, the trader believes that, at worst, implied volatility will stabilise over the next two months.
3. Interest rate differentials are too wide and will narrow over the same period.

The time spread exploits the fact that the time value of the option premium declines more rapidly over the last few weeks of its life than in the first few weeks; time decay is large on a day-to-day basis in options with under a month to expire, but is negligible for options of over three months' maturity. Therefore, selling the near and buying the far profits from this changing relationship. Any corresponding rise in implied volatility during this period will disproportionately increase the value of the medium- over the short-dated option; in a technical sense the theta is greater for the short-dated option and the vega is greater for the medium-

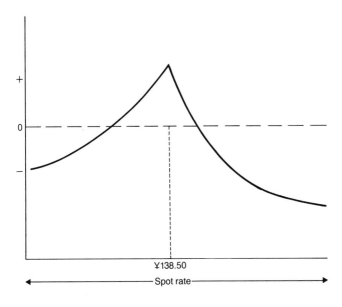

Write one billion yen 138.50 put for $0.000063
    Expiry : two months

Buy one billion yen 138.50 put for $0.000083
    Expiry : five months
    Volatility : 7 per cent
    $/yen interest rate differentials : 3.5 per cent

Spot rate	$ P/L after two months
149.27	(84,640)
148.12	(82,100)
146.99	(78,380)
145.87	(73,030)
144.77	(65,540)
143.68	(55,370)
142.61	(41,980)
141.56	(24,900)
140.52	(3,770)
139.50	21,630
138.50	51,180
137.50	32,740
136.52	18,060
135.56	6,690
134.61	(1,850)
133.67	(8,090)
132.74	(12,510)
131.83	(15,540)
130.93	(17,560)
130.04	(18,860)
129.17	(19,680)

Fig. 13.1   Calendar spread: Japanese yen.

dated option. Also the effects of the interest rate differential movement
through time – the gradual increase in the forward $/yen rate towards the
spot in stable conditions – will be amplified should the differential
actually narrow. In other words, over time, even unchanged interest rate
differentials will increase the value of the longer expiry option *vis-à-vis*
the shorter date; any narrowing of the differentials (lower US dollar
rates, or higher yen rates, or both) will have an effect of increasing the
value of the yen put option.

The trade is most profitable if the spot rate is close to the strike price on
the expiry of the short-dated option. Profitability can only be estimated,
but will be greater the higher the implied volatility of the outstanding
option and the narrower the interest rate differential (Fig. 13.2). Maximum loss is also an estimate, but assuming that interest rate differentials
and volatilities remain unchanged the greatest loss is the initial debit of
the transaction. The example of the sterling/Deutschmark option,
however, shows that a strong rally in the currency can lead to greater than
expected losses. However, when differentials are less extreme the potential for unforeseen losses is also lower.

The major disadvantage of time spreads lies in their inherent complexity. Usually it is difficult enough to gauge the likely direction of the
market over the medium term; indeed success in this field is generally
sufficient in itself without having recourse to use the option market. The
time spread requires a view of direction, volatility, and interest rate

Profit/loss profile of Fig 13.1 with volatility increasing to 9 per cent and interest rate
differential narrowing to 2.5 per cent

Spot rate	$ P/L after two months
149.27	(61,430)
148.12	(56,720)
146.99	(50,570)
145.87	(42,630)
144.77	(32,570)
143.68	(20,080)
142.60	(4,850)
141.56	13,360
140.52	34,770
139.50	59,540
138.50	87,470
137.50	66,550
136.52	48,760
135.56	33,850
134.61	21,560
133.67	11,600
132.74	3,670
131.83	(2,530)
130.93	(7,310)
130.04	(10,920)
129.17	(13,610)

Fig. 13.2   Calendar spread (2): Japanese yen.

differentials, and furthermore, a view limited to a particular horizon date. Nevertheless, it is an attractive strategy if it conforms to the particular view of the trader concerned.

Fence strategies

'Fences' are trades more commonly used by corporate treasurers or international investment managers to hedge their currency payables or receivables. Buying a call option, for example, and covering the premium by writing a put, is a useful trade for hedgers wishing to cover themselves against an upside move in the currency; on any sell-off the put will be assigned, which means that the treasurer will be 'given' the currency, but at a lower rate than the present spot or forward price and at probably a more beneficial level than his budgeted rate. For traders, too, the fence can be worthwhile, particularly if the trade takes advantage of attractive interest rate differentials. For example, in Fig. 13.3, with spot ECU at $1.15, a $1.17 six month ECU call is bought for $0.0230 and a $1.12 six month put written for the same premium. The trade has the advantage that because there is no net premium to pay, time decay is not an issue; if the ECU remains between $1.12 and $1.17 for the next six months there is no profit but neither is there any loss in the position. Also, again because the trade is for zero cost, the break-even level is the strike price of the call itself, not the strike plus the premium as with a simple option purchase. The trade-off is that, unlike a call purchase, there is no maximum loss if the market turns down. This problem can be avoided by adding a third leg to the fence.

The three-legged fence (see Fig. 13.4) is a combination of a long call and a short put (as with a normal fence) but with an added long put option to protect the position against a falling market. Again, the ideal trade is to put the three legs together for zero cost. The long call option ($1.5350) represents the level above which the trade moves into profit on expiry; because the construction is for no net premium cost the strategy will not lose money as long as spot is above $1.48 on expiry. Below this level, the loss is limited by the long $1.42 put option; thus the maximum loss will be 6 cents ($1.48 − $1.42). The transaction, therefore, has a similar exposure profile to the simple trade of call option buying (see Fig. 13.5) where the cost of a $1.50 call is only 4 cents. What, therefore, is the advantage of the three-legged trade when the potential cost is 50 per cent higher than with the simpler strategy? The answer is that the call option has to be paid for up-front, whereas the loss on the three-legged trade is only taken on expiry; secondly, the three-legged fence will be free as long as the spot is above $1.48, whereas the call option trade will only break even at $1.54. Finally, the loss on the three-legged trade is a maximum of

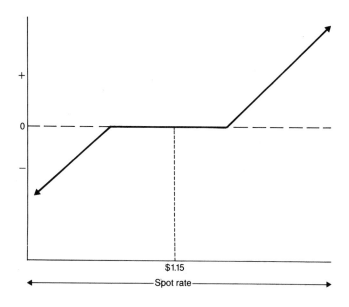

Buy one million ECU $1.17 call
  Premium : $0.023

Write one million ECU $1.12 put
  Premium : $0.023
  Expiry : six months

Spot rate	$ P/L at expiry
1.05	(70,000.00)
1.06	(60,000.00)
1.07	(50,000.00)
1.08	(40,000.00)
1.09	(30,000.00)
1.10	(20,000.00)
1.11	(10,000.00)
1.12	
1.13	
1.14	
1.15	
1.16	
1.17	
1.18	10,000.00
1.19	20,000.00
1.20	30,000.00
1.21	40,000.00
1.22	50,000.00
1.23	60,000.00
1.24	70,000.00
1.25	80,000.00

Fig. 13.3   Fence trade: ECU.

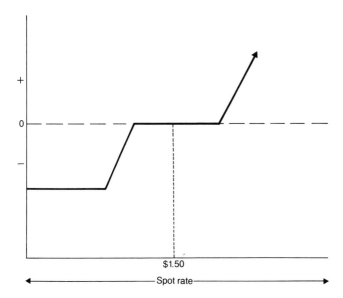

$1.50

Spot rate

Buy ten million sterling $1.5350 call for $0.025 cents

Write ten million sterling $1.48 put for $0.05 cents

Buy ten million sterling $1.42 put for $0.025 cents

Expiry : six months

Spot rate	$ P/L at expiry
1.30	(600,000.00)
1.32	(600,000.00)
1.35	(600,000.00)
1.36	(600,000.00)
1.38	(600,000.00)
1.40	(600,000.00)
1.42	(600,000.00)
1.44	(400,000.00)
1.46	(200,000.00)
1.48	
1.50	
1.52	
1.54	50,000.00
1.56	250,000.00
1.58	450,000.00
1.60	650,000.00
1.62	850,000.00
1.64	1,050,000.00
1.65	1,150,000.00
1.68	1,450,000.00
1.70	1.650,000.00

Fig. 13.4   'Three-legged fence': sterling.

Buy 10 million sterling $1.50 call for $0.04
  Expiry : six months

Spot rate	$ P/L at expiry
1.30	(400,000.00)
1.32	(400,000.00)
1.34	(400,000.00)
1.36	(400,000.00)
1.38	(400,000.00)
1.40	(400,000.00)
1.42	(400,000.00)
1.44	(400,000.00)
1.46	(400,000.00)
1.48	(400,000.00)
1.50	(400,000.00)
1.52	(200,000.00)
1.54	
1.56	200,000.00
1.58	400,000.00
1.60	600,000.00
1.62	800,000.00
1.64	1,000,000.00
1.66	1,200,000.00
1.68	1,400,000.00
1.70	1,600,000.00

Fig. 13.5   Buy call option: sterling.

6 cents, but it may be less; if the spot rate is at $1.46, for example, the loss is only 2 cents ($1.48 − $1.46).

A third variation on the fence trade is the ratio fence (see Fig. 13.6). Again the trade takes advantage of currency interest rate differentials which happen to be in the trader's favour. In the given example, with spot $/DM at DM 1.82, the trader who is bullish on the dollar buys a DM 1.87 put and writes a DM 1.82 call, both for three months; the difference is that the premium for the call ($0.012) is three times that of the put option ($0.004). Therefore, the trader can create a zero cost fence by buying three times as many puts as he writes calls (DM 30,000,000 1.87 puts to DM 10,000,000 1.82 calls). Again, the trade incurs no loss as long as the dollar is above the call strike of DM 1.82 on expiry; if the dollar is below DM 1.82 the loss profile is exactly the same as a short DM 10,000,000 spot position. But above DM 1.87 the position is long of DM 30,000,000 puts, with three times the potential leverage.

Cross-currency option trading

Inevitably, the main emphasis throughout this book has been on options on currencies against the US dollar; the vast majority of all spot, forward and options transactions, after all, are exclusively US dollar related. Yet a significant exposure exists for most internationally-trading corporations

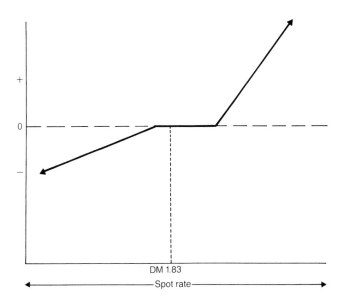

Buy 30 million Deutschmarks DM 1.87 puts
    Premium : $0.004

Write 10 million Deutschmarks DM 1.82 calls
    Premium : $0.012
    Expiry : three months

Spot rate	$ P/L at expiry
2.0446	1,370,000
2.0197	1,189,000
1.9954	1,008,000
1.9716	827,000
1.9484	646,000
1.9258	464,000
1.9036	283,000
1.8820	102,000
1.8608	
1.8402	
1.8200	
1.8002	(60,000)
1.7808	(120,000)
1.7619	(181,000)
1.7433	(241,000)
1.7252	(301,000)
1.7074	(362,000)
1.6900	(422,000)
1.6729	(483,000)
1.6500	(543,000)
1.6398	(603,000)

Fig. 13.6   Ratio fence: Deutschmarks.

on a cross-currency basis: the sterling rate against the Deutschmark is not only a vital factor for many British and West German companies, but for the Bank of England this particular cross-rate was probably more relevant than that of sterling against the US dollar in the six months preceding the General Election in May 1987. Other important cross-rates which are tied to international trade flows are the Japanese yen against sterling and against the Deutschmark. Also recent developments in international capital market trading have created new cross-currency exposures, many of them a direct result of attempts to exploit large interest rate differentials. Sterling against the Deutschmark and against the yen are again two obvious examples, but so are the Swiss franc and the Deutschmark against the Australian and New Zealand dollar. In the foreign exchange market itself, periods of stability in the US dollar based market has prompted greater trading interest in the crosses: inter-EMS trading, such as Deutschmarks against the Italian lira and the Belgian franc are two popular trades. Also, there is a tendency nowadays for currencies to be traded in 'blocs' rather than as separate units – the Asia/Pacific currencies of the newly industrialised countries (NICS) against the EMS, the EMS against the yen. It has even been popular to talk of the 'English speaking currencies' – the US, Canadian, Australian, and New Zealand dollar as well as the pound sterling – currencies which can be loosely connected by their higher inflation and interest rates, against other currency groups. This is all conducive to a greater awareness of inter-currency relationships rather than a simple US dollar based outlook.

One reason why no special mention was made of cross-currency options in the section on hedging was because, at bottom, options strategies for cross-currencies are the same as for the US dollar; there is no different method of covering the yen/Deutschmark risk than for the yen/US dollar risk. For trading techniques as well, strategies are the same for cross-currencies as for any other trading instrument. The only difference between a sterling call against the US dollar and a sterling call against Deutschmarks is that the former gives the holder the right to receive sterling in exchange for US dollars, and the latter gives the holder the right to receive sterling in exchange for Deutschmarks. The constituents of the option market, calls and puts, and the many permutations available for utilising these constituents, are the same for cross-currencies as for any other vehicle.

Unfortunately, this is not the whole picture; there are two serious problems in trading cross-rate options which are not evident when trading options against the US dollar. First of all, liquidity: in the same fashion as with the underlying spot and forward markets, spreads in the cross-rate option market are wider, and liquidity thinner, than with options against the US dollar; cross-rate options are only available in the over-the-counter market; there is no exchange traded option market in any 'cross'. Also, only a handful of banks will make markets in cross-rate options, and usually only for the more common crosses such as sterling/Deutschmark; trades are possible in the exotic cross-rates such as Swiss francs against New Zealand dollars but normally such transactions are only concluded through the matching up of counterparties. A secondary market in such options is virtually non-existent.

Secondly, and unlike the underlying spot or forward markets, it is impractical to create a cross-rate option through the US dollar. For example, with the spot sterling/dollar rate at $1.65, and the $/DM rate at DM 1.80, a long sterling/short Deutschmark spot cross-rate position can be established by trading both currencies against the dollar. Thus:

Sterling/$ rate: $1.65
$/DM rate: DM 1.80
1) Buy sterling at $1.65:   i.e. receive sterling 1 MM/deliver $1.65 MM
2) Buy $/DM at DM 1.80: i.e. receive $1.65 MM/deliver DM 2.97 MM
Net result: receive sterling 1,000,000 and deliver DM 2,970,000
or: buy sterling/DM at DM 2.97.

More simply, the cross-rate can be calculated by multiplying the two spot rates together:

Sterling/$1.65 × $/DM 1.80 = sterling/DM 2.97.

Given the existence of a sterling/Deutschmark option market a transaction might look as follows:

Expiry 3 months
Volatility 9 per cent
Spot sterling/DM 2.97
Strategy A: Buy sterling 1 million DM 2.97 call/Deutschmark put for 1.35 per cent or 4 pfennig.
Premium = sterling 13,500 or DM 40,000

Without a cross-rate option market, one method of creating such an option would be to buy a sterling/$ call, and a Deutschmark/$ put. Unfortunately, the volatility of a cross-rate currency is usually less than the volatility of its constituent parts. This makes the strategy of buying sterling calls and Deutschmark puts rather expensive:

Expiry: three months
Volatility: 12 per cent
Spot sterling: $1.65
Spot $/Deutschmark: DM 1.80

Strategy B: Buy sterling 1 million $1.65 call/$ put for 2.2 per cent or 3.6 cents.
(sterling 22,000 or $36,000)

Buy DM 2.97 million DM 1.80 put/$ call for 2.0 per cent or 3.6 pfennigs. ($33,000 or DM 59,400)

Total premium for strategy B: $69,000 or DM 124,000.

Alternatively, a 'synthetic' cross-rate option can be created by either buying a sterling call and writing a Deutschmark call option, or by buying a Deutschmark put and writing a sterling put option. The trade appears particularly attractive because it can be put on for a credit:

Strategy C: Buy sterling 1 million $1.65 call for 3.6 cents or $36,000/ write DM 2.97 million DM 1.80 call for 2.6 per cent or $43,000. Net credit: $7,000

Strategy D: Buy DM 2.97 million 1.80 put for 2.0 per cent or $33,000/ write sterling 1 million $1.65 put for 4.2 cents or $42,000. Net credit: $9,000.

However, the profit or loss exposure of these four strategies are not the same; given various movements in the two underlying spot rates, sterling/ US dollar and US dollar/Deutschmark, very different results will follow from apparently identical cross-rate movements.

Results on expiry:

1. Spot sterling $1.65
   Spot $/DM 1.80
   Spot sterling/Deutschmark: DM 2.97

   Profit/(loss) in US dollars
   Strategy A: ($22,275) (cross-rate option expires worthless)
   Strategy B: ($69,000) (both options expire worthless)
   Strategy C: $7,000 (both options expire worthless)
   Strategy D: $9,000 (both options expire worthless)

2. Spot sterling $1.50
   Spot $/DM: DM 1.98
   Spot sterling/Deutschmark: DM 2.97

   Profit/(loss) in US dollars
   Strategy A: ($22,275) (cross-rate option expires worthless)
   Strategy B: $81,000 (net loss on long sterling/$ call: $36,000 net profit on long DM 1.80 put: $117,000)
   Strategy C: $7,000 (both long $1.65 call and short DM 1.80 call expire worthless)
   Strategy D: $9,000 (net profit long DM 1.80 put: $117,000 net loss on short sterling 1.65 put: $108,000)

3. Spot sterling $1.80
    Spot $/DM: DM 1.65
    Spot sterling/DM: DM 2.97

    Profit/(loss) in US dollars

Strategy A: ($22,275) (cross-rate option expires worthless)

Strategy B: $81,000 (net profit on long sterling/$ call: $114,000
                        net profit on long DM 1.80 put: $33,000)

Strategy C: $7,000 (net profit on long sterling/$ call: $114,000
                        net loss on short DM 1.80 call: $107,000)

Strategy D: $9,000 (both short sterling $1.65 put and long DM 1.80 put
                        expire worthless)

When the spot cross-rate also moves the results will again vary substantially.

4. Spot sterling $1.50
    Spot $/DM: DM 1.80
    Spot sterling/DM: DM 2.70

    Profit/(loss) in US dollars

Strategy A: ($22,275) (cross-rate option expires worthless)

Strategy B: ($69,000) (both long $1.65 call and long DM 1.80 put expire
                        worthless)

Strategy C: $7,000 (both long $1.65 call and short DM 1.80 call expire
                        worthless)

Strategy D: ($141,000) (net loss on short $1.65 put: $108,000 long DM 1.80
                        put expires worthless)

5. Spot sterling $1.65
    Spot $/DM: DM 1.95
    Spot sterling/DM: DM 3.2175

    Profit/(loss) in US dollars

Strategy A: $105,000 (cross-rate option in-the-money by 24.75 pfennigs
                        per pound)

Strategy B: $58,000 (net profit on long DM 1.80 put: $94,000 long $1.65
                        call expires worthless)

Strategy C: $7,000 (both long $1.65 call and short DM 1.80 call expires
                        worthless)

Strategy D: $136,000 (short $1.65 put expires worthless
                        net profit on long DM 1.80 put: $94,000)

In conclusion it can be seen that a synthetic cross-rate option is a very different proposition from a straight option position; depending on the movement in the two underlying spot rates the profit or loss profile can vary widely. This is not necessarily a disadvantage, of course. Given a particular view of the cross-rate and of the two component spot rates, substantially greater profits can be made through the construction of a synthetic option position; the difference is that the risk/reward outlook is two-, rather than one-dimensional. It is yet another example of the almost infinite variety of trading strategies available through the currency options market.

PART FOUR

Conclusion

CHAPTER 14

The future for the currency options market

Some creations of the financial markets have the reputation of being ephemeral products, emerging overnight and fading away with little trace almost as quickly. When the currency options market opened in 1982 many traders questioned whether it, too, would be a nine days' wonder. Indeed, in the pioneering days of the Philadelphia Stock Exchange and during the first uncertain steps of the OTC market, it seemed that this product too, however well-intentioned, was unlikely to gain universal acceptance. But like other derivative markets, notably financial futures worldwide, the support of market-makers and the marketing efforts of the exchanges and the broking community, eventually paid dividends. Today the market is actively used around the clock and around the world by a wide-ranging trading sector; from private individuals to small and medium-sized corporations; from international investment managers to large multinationals; and from government agencies to the whole gamut of financial organisations, investment, merchant, and commercial banks.

The major question, now that the market can be said to have 'arrived', is where does it go from here? Of course, the danger of making predictions about such fast-developing products is that they tend to be out of date before they are even printed. Nevertheless, there are some definite trends emerging which are likely to push the currency options market into different directions in the future. The main stimulus behind new growth in the product is the international capital and equity markets. As long as financial barriers and trading frontiers continue to be pushed back, that is as long as the world does not move back into a protectionist environment, the increased accessibility of international markets can only lead to a greater demand for currency hedging products. As it becomes easier for fund managers to switch equity or bond portfolios, or for borrowers to tap different markets worldwide for funds, so the need to hedge the foreign exchange risk inherent in such transactions (which is often as great, and sometimes significantly greater than the interest rate or equity risk), becomes paramount. If the foreign exchange market stabilises for a period of months or years, then naturally the demand for hedging products – not just options, but spot and forward trading – will be reduced. But in all likelihood, the increase in trade and capital flows in addition to the trade imbalances between the major trading blocs, will ensure continued volatility in the markets. This said, where will the demand for risk management products, as far as currency options are concerned, lead the market? From recent developments this is likely to be in the longer end of the maturity range. Certainly the major development in the first months of 1987 was the greater trading activity in the long-dated currency options market. Where deals of over two years' maturity were considered exotic and highly specialised only six months before, by the second quarter of 1987 trades in large size of three to five year options were becoming almost commonplace.

The driving force behind this development was the bond market. Indeed, for much of 1985 and 1986 most of the novel concepts driving international capital market new issues were variations on the theme of long-dated currency options. The first development was the dual currency bond. In its basic form, this was a bond which paid interest in one currency, usually yen or Swiss francs, but redemption was in a different currency, usually US dollars. Usually, the coupon was higher than would normally be available in the Euro-yen or Euro-Swiss franc market but lower than in the 'straight' Eurodollar bond market.

Essentially, the lower US dollar coupon is equivalent to a premium which the investor pays for buying a dollar put option; in a stable to rising dollar environment the Eurodollar 'straight' will show the highest returns, but the dual-currency bond will outperform the straight yen or Swiss franc bond because of the higher currency coupon and the reduced foreign currency exposure. If the dollar declines the currency bond will perform best of all; but on a sharp dollar sell-off the dual-currency bond will outperform the straight Eurodollar bond because of the foreign exchange gain from the currency coupon payments. In other words, the exposure is very similar to buying a currency option for insurance purposes; the best strategy, with the benefit of hindsight, is either to buy the Eurodollar straight or the currency bond. The dual-currency bond is never the best strategy; but on any substantial move in the dollar its performance will be better than the worst strategy.

Other variations followed. In July 1986 Dai-Ichi Kangyo International brought an issue to the market for the Kingdom of Denmark which was dubbed the 'duet bond'; in this bond the coupon payment as well as the redemption amount varied according to the $/yen exchange rate. In October 1986, Nikko Securities lead managed a dual mixed-currency bond for Banque Nationale de Paris; interest payments were linked to the yen/New Zealand dollar exchange rate and redemption was 80 per cent in yen and 20 per cent in New Zealand dollars. In May 1985 American Medical International issued a $/Swiss franc dual-currency bond with equity warrants attached. The same year Minnesota Mining and Manufacturing Corporation issued the first dual-currency bond which paid interest in US dollars and principal in sterling. The majority of dual-currency bonds were $/yen based, however; 30 out of the 43 dual-currency issues in 1985 were in yen, 11 were in Swiss francs, and there was one issue each for sterling and Deutschmarks. So popular was the concept, indeed, that nearly $4 billion worth of dual currency bonds were issued in the year as a whole, and in one month, August 1985, dual-currency bonds accounted for 40 per cent of the total Euromarket volume.

However, the notion of a currency option actually embedded in a Eurobond was first developed by Credit Commercial de France. In April 1985 they had already re-opened the Euro-French franc bond market by lead managing a Ffr 500 million issue for Gaz de France. Later that year they brought out a US dollar floating rate note for Credit Foncier with the option to convert into a fixed rate 12.75 per cent French franc bond. In October and November warrants into Deutschmarks, Swiss francs, and ECU bonds followed: Electricité de France issued 40,000 warrants priced at $137.50 to buy bonds denominated in Swiss francs; CCF issued $250 million FRNs due 1994 with warrants, priced at $45, into a Deutschmark 6.375 per cent bond. CCF also lead managed a $75 million 6 year FRN for Union Bank of Norway with warrants into an ECU denominated 8.5 per cent bond; the warrants cost $37.50.

In October 1985, Bankers Trust lead managed a $100 million issue for the Long Term Credit Bank of Japan which they called an Indexed Currency Option Note, or 'ICON'. The principal of the ICON was that, in exchange for a currency risk, the investor received a higher coupon (in this case about 60 basis points) than was available in the Eurodollar 'straight' market. No alternative currency was offered at redemption or in interest payments; the bond was issued and redeemed in US dollars. But should a foreign exchange rate, the yen/dollar rate, be above a specific level at the maturity of the bond in ten years' time, the investor will receive a reduced principal payment on a sliding scale according to a predetermined formula. The specific FX rate, which acted like a strike price, was $/yen 169; the spot rate when the bond was issued was $/yen 210.

The formula was as follows:

Redemption value = [(1 – 169 – spot rate) ÷ spot rate] × face amount of notes

Thus as long as the US dollar was above yen 169 the bond would be redeemed for its full value; if it was below yen 169 on the redemption date, the value of the principal repayment would be reduced. See Table 14.1, for an example.

Essentially, the investor has written a ten year 169 yen call option to the borrower. While the spot $/yen rate was above yen 200 the risks seemed small and the issue was indeed well-received. But the sharp fall in the dollar throughout 1986 and the first half of 1987 (leaving the spot rate below yen 140 by May 1987) left the investor effectively short of a naked in-the-money currency call option (with eight years still remaining to expiry). No wonder that the ICON was soon re-christened the 'Heaven-and-Hell bond'. A variation on this theme was developed by Nomura International; they lead managed a $100 million issue for IBM which was split into two parts: a $50 million fixed- and $50 million floating rate note. Although the investor still suffered a lower redemption payment if the US dollar fell below yen 169, the advantage of this deal was that he also had the chance to gain a higher redemption amount if the dollar rallied; the structure of the issue was similar to a credit 'fence', where a yen call option is written and some of the proceeds used to purchase a yen put option. The investor will lose money (less his premium received which, in this case, is represented by the higher coupon), if the yen moves above the strike; if the yen remains inside a range he will gain by the extra coupon interest; if the yen falls below the strike of the put option the investor has the opportunity of making some profit on the trade.

In 1986 other currency option-linked products were introduced into the Euromarkets. The essential form was that of a conventional currency bond with currency warrants attached; they were attractive to investors who believed that the fall in the dollar was soon to reverse and therefore provided a two-way bet on the foreign exchange market: if the dollar continued to fall the investor benefited from owning the currency bond (less the 'premium' already paid for the warrant); if the dollar rallied the investor made a capital gain on his warrant to offset the foreign exchange loss on his currency bond. In this sense it was like a straddle or 'double

Table 14.1. Redemption values.

Spot $/yen at redemption	Redemption amount (%)
250	100
220	100
200	100
180	100
169	100
149	86
129	69
109	45
84.5	0

option'. The first such issue was brought to the market by Deutsche Bank for Deutsche Bank Finance NV (Curaçao). The issue was for a DM 400 million six year bond with a coupon of 6 per cent with two detachable warrants for each DM 5,000 bond. Warrant 'A' gave the investor the right to buy $500 and warrant 'B' the right to buy $2,000. This was followed by Trinkhaus and Burkhardt who lead managed a DM 100 million issue for the Council of Europe; the eight year bond had a coupon of 5.875 per cent and included a detachable warrant – effectively a three year US dollar call option on $500 struck at DM 1.78. Later, Morgan Stanley International brought a $100 million issue to the market for Scandinavian Airline System (SAS) which included detachable two year warrants to buy $500 at a strike price of DM 1.79.

Having whetted the appetite of retail investors for the currency warrant product the natural development in the market was to bring out naked currency warrants, that is warrants into a currency without any attachment to a host bond or in other words, a simple currency option under another name. Indeed the main differences between a warrant and an option is that a warrant is issued for longer maturity than in the exchange traded market (although not necessarily longer than the OTC market), a warrant is registered (usually in Luxemburg) and a secondary market is supported by the lead managers, but the principal difference is that the size of each warrant is normally much smaller than that of a currency option, either in the OTC market or on the exchanges. For example, in March 1987 Merrill International Bank Limited issued 200,000 warrants offering the investor the right to buy $500 at an exchange rate of DM 1.8150; the warrant was priced at $50 and the exercise period was for three years. In the terms of the currency options market it was a three year US dollar call/DM put struck at DM 1.8150 for a premium of 10 per cent. Thus the break-even exchange rate for the investor in three years' time was just below DM 2; given that the dollar had fallen by 50 per cent from a high of DM 3.45 since March of 1985, the chances of a reaction of at least 10 per cent from this sell-off made the warrant attractive in the eyes of the investor. The real attraction, however, was the fact that for the first time very small amounts and very long maturities, by the standards of the currency option market, were made available to the private investor. In this sense the naked warrant bridged the gap between the Euro-markets and the foreign exchange market.

Several naked currency warrants were issued at this time, some of which are shown in Table 14.2.

At the time that these currency related bonds were being brought to the markets, many observers were wondering whether they were 'just another wrinkle' introduced to make the issues more interesting, or whether they were to become a more permanent and integral part of the

Table 14.2. Currency warrant issues.

Issuer	No. of warrants	Strike	Price	Expiry
Banque indosuez	200,000	DM 1.79	$50	2 years
SEK	150,000	DM 1.79	$39	1.5 years
SEK	150,000	DM 1.79	$60	5 years
Citibank N.A.	100,000	DM 1.82	$39	2 years
DG Bank	200,000	STG/DM 2.74	STG 25	1.5 years
SBC Finance	200,000	SF 1.60	$36	2 years
Merrill Lynch	125,000	SF 1.567	$50	3 years
RBC (dollar calls)	100,000	Y 155	$34.5	2 years
RBC (dollar puts)	100,000	Y 145	$36.5	2 years

Euromarket structure. In terms of the international capital markets the case is not yet proven. But as far as the currency option market itself is concerned the question is almost irrelevant; the introduction of long-dated currency warrants and currency option related products gave the OTC market in particular a boost in a new direction. The attractions of the long-dated option market from a currency hedging point of view are clear when one considers the pricing of options of longer maturities. The fact that the option premium increases not in a linear fashion but in a ratio of the square root of time, that, for example, a twelve month option premium is not 12 times but only about three times that of a one month option, can make options with expiration dates two, three or four years hence look very attractive. In addition, the effect of interest rate differentials on an option's premium can appear to distort the cost of long-maturity options dramatically in favour of (but sometimes against) the option buyer. For example, Table 14.3 gives a comparison of theoretical premium values for yen call and put options, struck at the spot rate, with different maturities. The volatility is 13 per cent in each case.

Nowadays, the long-dated market has developed to such an extent that the only restriction on further expansion, either in size or maturity, lies with the underlying currency itself. Without a liquid forward foreign

Table 14.3. Comparison of theoretical premium values: yen call and put options.

Spot $/yen: Y 140	Theoretical option premiums (percentages): Expiration (years)				
	1	2	3	4	5
US $ rate (%)	7.75	8.0	8.0	8.5	8.5
Forward rate	Y 135	Y 130	Y 126	Y 121	Y 117
Yen 140 call	6.5%	9.8%	12.2%	15%	16.4%
Yen 140 put (Euro.)	3%	3.5%	3.5%	3.1%	3.0%

exchange market no effective long-dated currency option market can develop because the market-maker will be unable effectively to hedge his risk. Although counterparty-to-counterparty trading is always possible, this will do nothing to help develop depth in long-dated currency options trading; a secondary market will be non-existent in such circumstances. Thus the only way, for example, of quoting a five year option on Swiss francs against New Zealand dollars is for there to be a liquid forward market in the cross-currency; if the spreads in the forward market are very wide – which is the case with any long-date, not only the forward 'crosses' – the spreads in the option market will reflect this, and expansion of the market will be inhibited. Therefore, the next major area of development in currency options will depend on the ingenuity of market-makers themselves in being able to create alternative means of hedging in the long-dated foreign exchange market.

Other restrictions on the development of the currency options market are those of government and regulatory bodies. Until recently, Japanese corporations and investment funds, who probably had the greatest need world-wide for adequate currency hedging products, were not permitted to trade overseas exchanges or over-the-counter option markets. Many European investment and pension funds are prohibited by their trustees or by law from trading option markets, particularly from writing options. Similarly, the tax and legal treatment of derivative products, such as futures and options, in the United Kingdom and in West Germany has been at best confusing and at worst it has acted as a significant disincentive to potential users. However, in the same way that there has been a gradual trend towards the lifting of trade and capital flow barriers around the world, so the regulatory and accounting environment concerning currency option trading is slowly being liberalised. The growth in currency options trading is creating its own momentum; more and more, the demands for more suitable foreign exchange trading and hedging techniques by potential market users has forced a more flexible attitude on the part of market regulators.

The currency options market is no longer in its infancy. Whether for insurance purposes only, whether for more specific or strategic hedging requirements, or whether for exotic trading strategies, the market has the maturity and flexibility to suit the needs of all kinds of potential users. To quote the Philadelphia Stock Exchange once again, the currency options market has indeed become the third dimension to foreign exchange.

Glossary of terms

American option An option which may be exercised at any time.

At-the-money forward An option with an exercise price equal to the currency forward rate.

At-the-money spot An option with an exercise price equal to the currency spot rate.

Assignment Notification to the option writer requiring him to fulfil his contractual obligations to buy or sell the currency.

Bear spread An option strategy designed to allow the trader to participate, with limited profit and limited risk, in the decline of a currency.

Break-even point The foreign exchange rate or currency futures price at which a strategy neither makes nor loses money.

Bull spread An option strategy designed to allow the trader to participate, with limited risk and limited return, in the rise of a currency.

Butterfly spread A combination of a bull spread and a bear spread; the strategy normally gives a maximum return and maximum loss.

Call option An option which gives the holder the right to buy, and the writer the obligation to sell, a predetermined amount of a currency to a predetermined date at a predetermined exchange rate.

Calendar spread A strategy involving the buying and selling of options with different expiration dates.

Clearing house Organisation which matches and guarantees option trades on an exchange.

Combination See strangle.

Condor spread A variation on a butterfly spread but with strikes further apart.

Conversion arbitrage A riskless strategy involving the buying of a currency and the simultaneous buying of a put and writing of a call option, both normally European style and of the same strikes and expiration.

Covered write A strategy involving the buying of a currency and the writing of a call option, or the selling of a currency and the writing of a put option.

Credit The amount of money received when an option is written.

Debit The amount of money spent when an option is purchased.

Delta The ratio by which the price of the option moves relative to the underlying spot or futures contract.

Delta spread/delta trade/delta hedge A trade involving the adjustment of the long or short options positions by the ratio of the delta.

Discount Term used to describe an option trading for less than its intrinsic value.

Downside protection For covered calls the 'cushion' against loss provided by the option premium received.

Early exercise The exercise of an option before its expiration date.

Exercise Process by which the holder of an option elects to take delivery (call) or deliver (put) a currency according to the contract terms.

Exercise price The price at which the option holder has the right to buy or sell the underlying currency or currency futures contract.

Expiration date The last day on which a holder of an option can exercise.

Expiration time In the over-the-counter market the latest time an option may be exercised is usually 3.00 p.m. London time or 10.00 a.m. New York time, on that particular day.

European option An option which may only be exercised on the expiration day.

Exchange traded market Organised market-place for option trading purposes.

Expiration cycle In the exchange traded options market, the time frame in which listed options run.

Fair value Usually meaning value of an option premium according to a mathematical model.

Gamma The change in the delta for a unit change in the spot price.

Hedge ratio The ratio of options to buy or sell against a spot position in order to create a riskless hedge. See 'delta'.

Implied volatility The expected standard deviation of percentage price changes.

In-the-money An option that has intrinsic value. For a call, the strike is below the spot rate; for a put, the strike is above the spot rate.

Intrinsic value Value of an option were it to be exercised immediately.

Leg One component of a multiple option strategy.

Margin Initial margin is amount required to be put up as collateral by the clearing house from option writers. Equivalent to a performance bond. Variation or maintenance margin is further cover required should the option position move against the writer.

Mark to market Daily adjustment of an account to reflect accrued profits and losses.

Money spread Strategy involving the buying and writing of options with different strikes but with the same expiration dates. Can be put on for a credit or debit to take advantage of a directional market move.

Naked position A short option position which is not covered by the underlying currency or with another option.

Out-of-the-money An option with no intrinsic value. For a call, the strike is above the spot rate; for a put the strike is below the spot rate.

Over-the-counter market Customised option market usually traded directly between banks and their customers or with other banks.

Premium Amount of money paid by a buyer or received by a seller, for an option.

Put option An option giving the holder the right to sell, and the writer the obligation to buy, a predetermined amount of currency to a predetermined date at a predetermined exchange rate.

Ratio spread Strategy involving the sale of an amount of call options in excess of the amount of a long call option position held, or the sale of put options in excess of the amount of a long put option position held.

Ratio write Strategy involving the sale of call options in excess of the amount of a long currency position held, or the sale of put options in excess of the amount of a short currency position held.

Reversal arbitrage Riskless trade involving the selling of a currency and the simultaneous buying of a currency call and writing of a currency put option, both normally European style and of the same strikes and expiration.

Settlement date Two business days following exercise; the day on which the currencies involved in the option transaction are exchanged.

Spread Strategy involving the simultaneous buying and selling of options on the same currency.

Straddle Strategy involving the buying of call and put options with the same strikes and maturity.

Strangle Strategy involving the buying of call and put options with different strikes but with the same expiration dates.

Strike See 'exercise price'.

Theta The change in the premium for a unit change in time.

Time value The amount by which an option premium exceeds its intrinsic or 'in-the-money' value.

Volatility The standard deviation of percentage price changes.

Vega The change in the premium for a unit change in implied volatility.

Writer One who sells an option.

Bibliography

F. Black, 'Fact and fantasy in the use of options', *Financial Analysts Journal*, vol. 31 (January/March 1976), pp. 167–91.

F. Black and M. Scholes, 'The pricing of options and corporate liabilities', *Journal of Political Economy*, (May/June 1973), pp. 637–54.

R. M. Bookstaber, *Option Pricing and Strategies in Investing*, Addison-Wesley, (1981).

G. Chamberlain, *Trading in Options*, Woodhead-Faulkner, 2nd edition, (1986).

Chicago Board of Trade, *Basic spread strategies*.

Chicago Board of Trade, *Opportunities in Options on US Treasury Bond Futures*, (1982).

Chicago Board of Trade, *Strategies for Buying and Writing Options: a Reference Guide for Profit-seeking Investors*, (1982).

Chicago Mercantile Exchange, *Currency Options Strategy Manual*, (1984).

Chicago Mercantile Exchange, *Market Perspectives*.

J. C. Cox and S. Ross, 'The valuation of options for alternative stochastic processes', *Journal of Financial Economics*, vol. 3, (1976), pp. 145–66.

J. C. Cox and M. Rubinstein, 'Option pricing: a simplified approach', *Journal of Financial Economics*, vol. 7, (1979), pp. 229–63.

Futures and Options World, London: various articles.

V. Gadkari, *Relative Pricing of Currency Options*, Salomon Brothers Inc., (1983).

V. Gadkari and B. Brittain, *An Introduction to Currency Options*, Salomon Brothers Inc., (1983).

M. Garman and Steven W. Kolhagen, *Foreign Currency Option Values*, School of Business Administration, University of California, (December 1982).

G. Gastineau, *The Stock Options Manual*, McGraw-Hill, (1979).

Intermarket magazine, Chicago: various articles.

L. McMillan, *Options as a Strategic Investment*, New York Institute of Finance, (1986).

J. Meisner and J. Labuszewski, 'Modifying the Black–Scholes option pricing model for alternative underlying instruments', *Financial Analysts Journal*, vol. 40 (Nov.–Dec. 1984).

Merrill Lynch Capital Markets, *Currency Options Strategy Guide*, Financial Futures and Options Group, (1986).

Philadelphia Stock Exchange Publications, *Foreign Currency Options*.

Index

American style options, 27, 45–7, 48–54
Amsterdam *see* EOE
arbitrage, 28, 45, 46, 66–70

back-to-back loans, 73
backspread, 169–70, 174–5
binomial model, 56–7
Black–Scholes model, 55–65
Boston option, 93
break-forward, 93
Bretton Woods, 73
butterfly spread, 159, 163, 164

calendar spread, 177–83
call option buying, 143–51
  follow-up action, 146–51
capital markets, 196–201
CAPO, 93
CBOE (Chicago Board Options
    Exchange), 9, 55
Chicago, 2, 7, 9, 11, 20, 54
clearing house, 12–14, 18
CME *see* IOM
compound options, 94
condor spread, 163
Cox–Ross–Rubinstein model, 56–7
credit spread, 156
cross-currency options, 176–8, 186–91
currency options definitions, 2, 22, 27, 28,
    47, 48, 54
currency risk, 73, 74–6
currency warrants, 199–200

deferred premium options, 93
delta, 60–1
delta trading, 137, 138, 142, 169, 173,
    174–5
derivative products, 1, 2
derivatives of the option pricing model,
    60–6
dual currency bond, 196–7

EMS, 33, 58–9
EOE (European Options Exchange,
    Amsterdam), 7, 9
European style options, 27, 45–7
exchange traded options markets, 7–20
exercise of options, 27–8, 48–54

fence trading, 183–7
foreign exchange quotation
  European style, 22–7
  reciprocal style, 21–7
forward conversion, 67
forward exchange market, 59, 73, 76–8,
    88
  hedging, 76–8, 88, 96, 110
forward reversal, 67
FXFG, 93

gamma, 61–2
Garman–Kholhagen model, 56–7
gearing *see* leverage
gilts, 1, 108–15

Heaven and Hell bond *see* ICON
hedge ratio *see* delta
hedging (currency options), 71–122
  advantages of options, 84–5
  butterfly hedge, 108
  disadvantages of options, 81–2
  fence hedge, 87, 89, 90, 91, 104–7,
    111–12
  fixed income investments, 75–6,
    108–15
  option buying, 76–82, 88, 89, 96, 97–9,
    110
  option writing, 86–92, 99–104, 111,
    116–22
  packaged products, 92–4
  rolling down, 116–17
  rolling out, 119–22
  rolling up, 117–18, 146, 148, 149